Basic Concepts
of
Swaminarayan
Satsang

Basic Concepts
of
Swaminarayan
Satsang

Translated by:
Sadhu Vivekjivandas
Sadhu Amrutvijaydas

SWAMINARAYAN AKSHARPITH
Ahmedabad

Basic Concepts of Swaminarayan Satsang

Translated by: Sadhu Vivekjivandas, Sadhu Amrutvijaydas

Inspirer: HDH Pramukh Swami Maharaj

First Edition: May 2002
First Reprint: May 2003
Second Reprint: May 2007

Copies: 3,000 (Total: 9,000)
Cost: Rs. 25.00
ISBN: 81-7526-200-1

Published & Printed by
Swaminarayan Aksharpith
Shahibaug, Ahmedabad-4, India

Websites: www.swaminarayan.org
www.akshardham.com
www.mandir.org
kids.baps.org

CONTENTS

CONTENTS

PREFACE

Bhagwan Swaminarayan (1781-1830) established a unique and eternal path of spiritual endeavour for all aspirants desiring *moksha* or liberation. He prescribed the ultimate goal of attaining realisation by imbibing the virtues of *dharma, gnan, vairagya* and *bhakti* – collectively called *ekantik dharma*. To integrate these four fundamental virtues, Bhagwan Swaminarayan clearly defined the components of spiritual *sadhana* in His teachings, compiled in the Vachanamrut.

This new publication, 'Basic Concepts of Swaminarayan Satsang', published through the inspiration of His Divine Holiness Pramukh Swami Maharaj, includes references from the Vachanamrut and teachings of Gunatitanand Swami, substantiated with lucid incidents that reveal the spirit of the subjects concerned. The *sadhana* or spiritual endeavours described in this book do not deal with the rituals and practices in the Swaminarayan Sampraday, but the fundamental elements necessary for internal understanding and realisation to make the external practices more profound and fruitful.

Reading and reflecting upon every chapter will consolidate one's understanding and knowledge about the basic concepts of Swaminarayan Satsang and add momentum to imbibing these redemptory virtues.

This book is a translation of the Gujarati version called 'Satsang Samjan'. It has 100 references from the Vachanamrut, 18 from Swamini Vato, 18 verses and 68 stories. The diacritic ā has been used only in direct quotations from the Vachanamrut, Swamini Vato and verses. Elsewhere, including the glossary, no diacritics have been used.

We hope this small publication will be a beacon of inspiration to all devotees and aspirants on the path of spiritual enlightenment.

Publishers
Swaminarayan Aksharpith

1. SERVICE

One should serve God and His devotee with body, mind and spirit. Service means to serve with glory and with the motive to please God only.

1. *In order to please God, I desire only to serve devotees of God in this life and all subsequent lives. Furthermore, just as this is My resolution, all of you should also make the same resolution.*

   - Vachanāmrut Gadhadā II-28

2. *Just as Ukā Khāchar has become addicted to serving the sadhus, in the same way, if one becomes addicted to serving God and His Sant to the extent that one would not be able to stay for even a moment without serving them, then all of the impure desires in one's antahkaran will be destroyed.*

   -Vachanāmrut Gadhadā II-25

3. *Only those who have accumulated a great number of merits from performing good deeds receive the opportunity to serve God's Sant, but those who have a few merits do not.*

   -Vachanāmrut Gadhadā II-59

4. *By performing with extreme affection such similar service of God and the Sant who possesses the highest qualities, even if he is a devotee of the lowest type and was destined to become a devotee of the highest type after two lives, or after four lives, or after ten lives, or after 100 lives, he will become a devotee of the highest calibre in this very life. Such are the fruits of the similar service of God and God's Bhakta.*

   -Vachanāmrut Vartāl-5

5. *Real worth lies in two things: in serving God and His Devotee.*

   Swāmini Vāto: 5.347

Story 1

These Mango Trees Are Drying up

Once, Aksharmurti Gunatitanand Swami arrived at the village of Maliya. The enthusiastic local devotees had arranged a festival in a mango grove. When Swami came to the mango grove he said, "Without water these mango trees are drying up."

Pragji Bhakta heard Gunatitanand Swami's words. Perceiving his inner wish, he immediately began watering the trees. He took two empty pots to the river, filled them with water and emptied them by each tree. In this way he served four potfuls of water to every tree. After several hours, when Pragji Bhakta finished the task of watering 300 mango trees, he was drenched with water and sweat.

Then Pragji Bhakta came to Gunatitanand Swami. On seeing him wet, Gunatitanand Swami was immensely pleased at his *seva* and said, "Doing service or *seva* according to the inner wish (of the guru) is *bhakti*."

The devotees realised the importance of the unique *seva* performed by Pragji Bhakta.

Story 2

Not Rejecting Seva

Pramukh Swami Maharaj was in the village of Undhela, in Kheda district, Gujarat. After making home-visits all morning, Swamishri began replying to letters in the afternoon. Though it was time to rest, Swamishri kept on writing one letter after another. Then an attendant sadhu came and placed another pile of letters. Swamishri was absorbed in his correspondence. A sadhu seated in the room could no longer restrain himself and thus placed his hand on the pile of letters and said, "Swami, please stop now. You can answer these letters later.

You have been writing for quite some time." But Swamishri did not pay any attention.

The sadhu humbly requested, "Bapa! Answer these letters later. You will get tired. It would be better if you take some rest now."

Swamishri smiled at the sadhu and said, "This is *seva*. *Seva* should not be rejected." And Swamishri continued answering the letters.

In the last three decades Swamishri has read and written 500,000 letters. He never tires answering the unending torrent of letters he receives each day. Neither old age nor his hectic travelling schedules or daily agenda of work prevents him from this *seva*. He sees this *seva* as a service to God and that is why he never neglects it.

Story 3

Used Datan Sticks

In 1971, the 51st birthday celebration of Pramukh Swami Maharaj was organised in Dharmaj. The sadhus and devotees were eager and excited about the celebration. On the morning of the birthday celebration, Swamishri was brushing his teeth with a *datan*. He noticed used *datans* lying outside a nearby dustbin. Many devotees had brushed their teeth earlier and, out of negligence, thrown them outside the bin. After brushing his teeth, Swamishri picked up all the dirty *datans* with his own hands and put them in the bin.

Swamishri could have told someone to pick up the *datans* and throw them in the bin, but he humbly performed the service himself. Though it was his birthday, he did not hesitate in doing the *seva* himself.

Swamishri's spirit of *seva* and humility is an inspiring message for all to dedicate themselves in doing *seva*.

2. SPIRITUAL COMMAND

A command or *agna* is a moral and spiritual injunction prescribed by God, Satpurush and the scriptures.

1. *Only one who follows the commands of the Satpurush is behaving as the* ātmā.

   - Vachanāmrut Gadhadā II-51

2. *Although at the time there may not seem to be any benefit in observing the moral do's and don'ts, one who does observe* dharma *by the command of a great Purush ultimately attains liberation – just as one receives cash from drafts.*

   - Vachanāmrut Gadhadā II-6

3. *For a devotee of God, whatever misery he suffers is due to negligence in observing God's injunctions for the sake of worthless objects; and whatever happiness he experiences is a result of following the injunctions of God.*

   - Vachanāmrut Gadhadā I-34

4. *All of the* indriyas *and* antahkaran *tremble with fear before a devotee who has courage. Also, he is not afraid of anyone. So, he does not transgress any of God's injunctions in any way.*

   - Vachanāmrut Loyā-2

5. *Greater is he who merely sits or does only what he is told by the holy sadhu than he who wilfully does the work of two people.*

   - Swāmini Vāto: 1.109

Story 1

Four Devotees of Memka

Mulji Sheth, a disciple of Bhagwan Swaminarayan, resided in the village of Memka. Once he requested Shriji Maharaj to come and bless his village.

Shriji Maharaj was pleased by Mulji Sheth's love and affection and consented to his wish and asked him to make preparations for His visit.

Mulji Sheth happily returned to Memka and made the necessary preparations for Maharaj's reception. Shriji Maharaj arrived with a large following of sadhus and devotees.

The other *satsangi* residents of the village were Hansraj Suthar, Shamo Aagolo and Shamo Kansagaro. They all served Maharaj and the entire group for three days.

On the day of departure, Shriji Maharaj called the four devotees and instructed, "Within twenty days leave this village and settle elsewhere." The four devotees were surprised at Maharaj's words. But since it was His command, they left Memka with their belongings.

On the twenty-first day, the Gaekwad's army, led by Babaji, looted the entire village. The four devotees who had obeyed the command of Maharaj were safe and sound.

God protects those who obey His commands.

Story 2

Satpurush's Command

Once Yogiji Maharaj was at the Dadar mandir in Mumbai. Many aspirants and devotees would come for his *darshan* and seek his blessings. A devotee, once, brought his *bania* friend along with him. The new aspirant had observed *dharna-parna* for 13 months, which involved fasting on alternate days and eating only once on the following day. Yogiji Maharaj was pleased at the aspirant's accomplishment and happily blessed him. After he left, Yogiji Maharaj addressed the devotees, "If anyone were to fast for only one day by the commands of the Satpurush, then he would receive the fruits equal to a year's observance of *dharna-parna!*"

Obedience to even the smallest commands of the Satpurush merits one with the highest and greatest fruit.

Story 3

"Go and Call Girnar."

Gunatitanand Swami was seated in the assembly hall of Junagadh mandir. Hundreds of devotees were absorbed in Swami's discourse. Swami suddenly called Pragji Bhakta and instructed him, "Go and call Girnar, the mountain. For years it has been performing austerities. I want to bless it with the fruits of its austerity."

Everyone was surprised at this command, but Pragji Bhakta immediately departed to call Girnar. Then a devotee asked him, "Listen Pragji! Swami has told you to call Girnar, but how can the mountain come!"

The obedient Pragji replied with a ring of faith, "On Swami's command I will go and tell Girnar, 'Come, Swami is calling you.' If it does not come then it will have disobeyed; but I must obey his command!"

A true devotee does not hesitate or doubt in following the command of God or the guru.

3. ACCEPTING GOOD QUALITIES

Looking at and imbibing the virtues of God, Satpurush and devotees tantamount to appreciating their qualities.

1. *Just as Dattātreya imbibed the virtues of the five* bhuts, *the moon, various animals, a prostitute, a virgin, his own body and others, similarly, only if a person has the disposition of imbibing the virtues of a sadhu does his foundation in Satsang become solid.*

   - Vachanāmrut Loyā-5

2. *A person who is wise increasingly finds flaws within himself and perceives virtues in God and His devotees.*

   - Vachanāmrut Gadhadā I-6

3. *The more one continues to imbibe the virtues of the great Purush, the more one's* bhakti *begins to flourish. In fact, if one realises the truly great Purush to be absolutely lust-free, then, even if one is as lustful as a dog, one will also become lust-free. Conversely, if one perceives the fault of lust in the great Purush, then no matter how lust-free one may be, one becomes full of intense lust. In the same manner, if one views the great Purush to be full of anger or avarice, then one becomes full of anger and avarice. Therefore, if one understands the great Purush to be absolutely free of lust, avarice, taste, egotism and attachment, one will also become free of all of those evil natures and become a staunch devotee.*

   - Vachanāmrut Gadhadā I-58

4. *Sing the glory of God's Devotee; by this the* jiva *can become* brahmarup *effortlessly.*

   - Swāmini Vāto: 4.140

Story 1

A Single Virtue from Everyone

Once Shriji Maharaj came to serve food to the sadhus. He served lovingly and filled their bowls to the brim. The sadhus hailed the name of Maharaj for being blessed with food served by His own hands. As they were about to commence their meals, two sadhus arrived. They had not eaten either.

Maharaj was aware that there were no food items left to serve. How would He fill their bowls now?

So Shriji Maharaj told them, "Go to all the sadhus with your eating bowls and ask for a little food from everyone."

The two sadhus held their bowls before every sadhu, and each one in turn gave them the best item they had. Within no time their bowls were full and the sadhus joined the group.

On seeing this, Shriji Maharaj told a moral to the sadhus, "Listen everyone! The bowls of these two sadhus were initially empty. But when they bent low to accept what you gave, their bowls became full with the best food items. Similarly, in Satsang, if you humbly accept a single virtue from everyone then your life will become full of virtues."

By accepting the good qualities of others, one's life becomes virtuous and divine. A little pledge to see and accept the virtues of others will enrich one's heart with the joys of goodness and divinity.

Story 2

Ninety-nine Faults, but One Virtue!

In 1984, Pramukh Swami Maharaj was in Antwerp, Belgium. In a small congregation someone asked Swamishri, "We experience friction or personality clashes while engaged in Satsang activities. Consequently, we see faults in the persons concerned. You are aware of everyone's fault, yet how do you see us?"

Swamishri spontaneously replied, "God and the holy Sadhu do not look at the faults of others. On seeing them one should turn blind; on hearing them one should turn deaf; and on knowing them one should remain silent. Even if a person has ninety-nine faults, he must have one virtue! So always see that one virtue!"

The holy great always focus in perceiving the virtues of people. They appreciate a small virtue a thousand-fold more than what it is worth.

Story 3

Removed His Affinity for Tasty Food

Devotees from far and wide came to Junagadh to listen to Gunatitanand Swami's discourses.

A Nagar Brahmin of Junagadh came daily for Swami's *darshan*. Though he lived a comfortable life, he had a weakness for delicious food. He loved eating hot chapattis. And whenever his meals were cold or tasteless, he would react angrily. Every day his wife and mother would remain nervous till he finished his meals.

Once, the Nagar Brahmin went for Gunatitanand Swami's *darshan*. After the discourse, Swami went to have lunch in the sadhus' dining hall. The Nagar Brahmin thought, "Though I am an ordinary person I still get tasty meals to eat. And Gunatitanand Swami, being the Mahant of the mandir, must be having delicious food for lunch and dinner!" And with this thought the Brahmin followed Swami and waited at a respectable distance to see what he would be eating. First, the attendant came and served a crushed form of millet chapatti. The Brahmin thought some sweet item had been placed. Then he saw the attendant pour what seemed like milk. He was convinced that Swami was eating an excellent sweet item. However, when Gunatitanand Swami asked for some salt, he realised it was not milk but buttermilk that had been served in his bowl. On coming nearer, Gunatitanand Swami revealed to

him, "I am not eating what you have in mind. It is only crushed
rotlo and buttermilk. Now I shall add salt, mix it together and
have it." The Brahmin was amazed and felt, "Though Swami is
the *mahant* of such a big mandir he eats only a simple meal!"

On appreciating Swami's virtue of non-taste, the Brahmin's
intense desire for tasty food disappeared. Thus by appreciating
the virtues of the holy Sadhu, one is redeemed of all desires
and base nature.

4. SPIRITUAL DISCOURSES

Talks on the divine episodes of God and the Satpurush or discussions or explanations based on scriptures and topics related to religion are known as spiritual discourses (*katha*).

1. *One develops an aversion for the world in proportion to the attachment one has for listening to the talks and discourses related to God; moreover, vicious natures such as lust, anger, avarice, etc., are also destroyed to that extent. Conversely, if someone is lazy in listening to those talks and discourses, then one should infer that he will not imbibe noble virtues.*

   - Vachanāmrut Gadhadā III-24

2. *Moreover, the mind does not become as free of desires for vishays by subjecting the body to austere observances such as tapta-kruchchh, chāndrāyan or other vows as it does by listening to these discourses of God. In addition, your minds must not be becoming as stable while meditating or by turning the rosary as perfectly as they do while you are listening to these discourses. Thus, one should listen to the discourses of Purushottam Nārāyan with faith and love. There is no better method to stabilise the mind and to free it of the desires for vishays.*

   - Vachanāmrut Kariyāni-12

3. *One should only hear the sacred scriptures from a holy person, but never from an unholy person.*

   - Vachanāmrut Loyā-11

4. *My mind never becomes satiated with spiritual discourses, devotional songs, talks related to God or meditation of God. All of you should also do the same.*

   - Vachanāmrut Gadhadā II-49

5. *One should forgo the profit of Rs. 25,000 and attend the Sunday assembly.*

- Yogiji Maharaj

Story 1

Faith in Discourses

Once Shriji Maharaj was in Gadhada. Every day, in the morning, afternoon, evening and late at night, He discoursed to the congregation. The *paramhansas* faithfully and untiringly listened to Maharaj's divine discourses. Aksharbrahma Gunatitanand Swami became engrossed and overwhelmed with bliss while he listened to His sermons.

One evening, after *arti*, Maharaj commenced His discourse. As He talked, Maharaj became so absorbed that He lost all sense of time. When Shriji Maharaj realised that it was 3 am He stopped and told the *paramhansas*, "It is quite late now. I shall continue my discourse later in the morning. You may now all go and rest."

At that time Gunatitanand Swami humbly requested Maharaj, "If you are telling us to go for rest then we are experiencing peace and rest in Your discourses. Therefore, please continue Your sermons." Shriji Maharaj was pleased with Gunatitanand Swami's faith and inclination towards discourses. Maharaj continued His wonderful discourse and satisfied the *paramhansas*.

By listening to spiritual discourses with love and faith one's frustrations and miseries are dissolved, one's heart and mind become pure and one's soul rejoices in the eternal joys of God.

Story 2

A Deal in Chaff

Aksharbrahma Gunatitanand Swami had arranged a schedule of round-the-clock discourses in Junagadh mandir. Eight *puranis* would keep the assembly hall resonating day and night with their scriptural readings. Many devotees of the Sorath region would stay in Junagadh to listen to the discourses. Shivlal Sheth of Botad, a wealthy businessman, unfailingly stayed for at least a month every year to listen to Gunatitanand Swami's discourses.

Once, in the afternoon, Shivlal went off to the bazaar in Junagadh. After buying and selling a little gold, he profited a sum of Rs.150. When he returned to the mandir, he informed Swami about his lucrative deal and said, "I donate the Rs.150 for the purpose of offering lunch to Thakorji and the sadhus!"

But Gunatitanand Swami was not pleased with Shivlal for having left the discourse to go to the bazaar. "Shivlal, can you ever dream of doing the business of selling 20 billion kilos of chaff?"

"No, Swami! "How can one ever engage in such a business?" Shivlal replied.

Then Gunatitanand Swami pointed out, "By leaving the discourse to do business in the bazaar is like selling 20 billion kilos of chaff. If you had spent that time listening to a sadhu's discourse you would have benefited many times over."

In the eyes of the holy Sadhu, mundane things are like dust in comparison to the glory of spiritual discourses.

Story 3

The Atma Becomes Weak!

In 1982, Pramukh Swami Maharaj was recuperating from an illness in Sarangpur. Once, after lunch, Swamishri took hold of a *parshad's* hand for support and started walking. Swamishri unexpectedly turned in the direction of the assembly hall where a scripture was being read during the afternoon assembly.

The *parshad* requested, "Swamishri, do not go to the discourse. It will be better if you rest. Where is the need for you to listen to the discourse?"

But Swamishri replied with conviction, "One has to attend the discourse, otherwise the atma will become weak."

For Swamishri, spiritual discourses are a source of rest and recovery. Spiritual discourses are the food for the *atma*. Through them, Satsang flourishes. And to strengthen one's inner self, spiritual discourses are essential and indispensable.

5. TOLERANCE

Tolerance is to forgive others and bear hardships.

1. *Since it is God who resides in all of the indriyas of such a Sant, that Sant is able to empower the indriyas of all beings in the brahmānd. Therefore, such a Sant is the sustainer of the world. His greatness lies in the fact that he tolerates the insults delivered even by insignificant people. Only those who are forgiving in this manner should be considered to be extremely great.*

- Vachanāmrut Gadhadā I-27

2. *If that Sant were to daily beat him five times with a pair of shoes, he should still tolerate such insults, but just as an opium addict cannot abandon his addiction, in no way should he abandon his association with the Sant. Such a person should be known to be equal to the Sant mentioned earlier. Moreover, whatever that Sant attains, one who continues to profoundly associate with such a Sant also attains.*

- Vachanāmrut Sārangpur-10

3. *Gālidānam tādanam cha krutam kumatibhirjanaihi Kshantavyam eva sarveshām chintaniyam hitam chh taihi.*

- Shikshāpatri: 201

"They (sadhus) shall always bear the abuses and insults hurled upon them by the wicked and also their beatings. Such acts should always be forgiven and the persecutors blessed for a betterment in their life."

4. *Tolerate praises and insults. One who tolerates is ekāntik.*

- Yogiji Maharaj

5. *When an aspirant is scolded he becomes happy. The virtue of tolerance is indispensable for one who wants liberation.*

- Pramukh Swami Maharaj

Story 1

A Favour in Return for Persecution

Gunatitanand Swami was touring the Sorath region with a group of Sadhus. In some villages, where the devotees resided, they were honoured and welcomed; whereas in others the unfriendly folks insulted and persecuted them.

Once, Gunatitanand Swami arrived at the village of Juna Savar. Uga Khuman, the village chief, loathed the Swaminarayan sadhus. On hearing the news of their arrival, Uga Khuman became inflamed with anger. He and his men insulted them, thrashed them and drove them out of the village.

The sadhus unresistingly hobbled their way to the village lake. The extent of their persecution was evident from their bleeding wounds and sore bodies. When the village women came to fill their pots with water they were moved by the wanton cruelty meted out to the sadhus by the village chief. Out of compassion they uttered, "How can God bless the Darbar with a child when he persecutes such innocent sadhus! Such a merciless village chief shall always remain childless."

When Gunatitanand Swami came to know of this, he and the sadhus prayed to Shriji Maharaj to bless the Darbar with a child and thereafter to have his house graced by sadhus.

And Gunatitanand Swami's prayers were answered. Even at an old age Uga Khuman fathered a baby boy. Several years later, when Gunatitanand Swami was passing through the outskirts of Juna Savar, Uga Khuman's eight-year old boy caught hold of Swami's finger and brought him and the sadhus home. Gunatitanand Swami reminded Uga Khuman, "Darbar! Do you remember that several years ago you had beaten us and expelled us from this village! However, on hearing that you were childless, we prayed to Shriji Maharaj to bless you with a son. And by the grace of Swaminarayan you have been blessed with this boy."

Uga Khuman repented for his ruthless act and prayed for forgiveness.

One who blesses in return for persecution is a sadhu. Gunatitanand Swami was fearless because he considered no one to be his enemy. He had sowed the seeds of *Satsang* by tolerating innumerable occasions of insult, pain and persecution. Today, those seeds have grown into giant banyan trees, providing solace to innumerable souls.

Story 2

Insult in Anand

Once Shriji Maharaj visited the town of Anand. The local devotees had enthusiastically made preparations for a welcome procession. Maharaj had arrived with a group of *paramhansas* and armed Kathi devotees. Before the procession commenced, Maharaj sought a pledge from the Kathi devotees, "Do not use your swords or weapons, even if anyone insults us, throws bricks or flings mud at us. Instead, forgive them."

Shriji Maharaj's foreboding words sparked off a flurry of thoughts in everyone's mind. And Maharaj's words came true. Many of the hostile people of Anand insulted Maharaj and his company of *sadhus* and devotees. They bitterly hurled mud, bricks, stones, dung and rubbish as the procession passed through the town centre.

The Kathi devotees suppressed their anger and ferocity and tamely tolerated the affront. Though their hearts boiled and itched with a desire to retaliate, they abided by their pledge to Maharaj. Shriji Maharaj left Anand and arrived in Vartal. Here, Maharaj assembled the congregation by the banks of Gomti lake. Everyone looked crestfallen and moodless. Maharaj then addressed the assembly, "Today we have won the citadel of Idar. Through tolerance we have enhanced our pride and reputation." Maharaj's words calmed their agitated minds.

God is compassionate and merciful. He tolerates everyone. Shriji Maharaj had emphasised tolerance as a great virtue. He imbibed the virtue in His life and prescribed tolerance for all His devotees!

Story 3

Serving an Opponent

Yogiji Maharaj arrived in the village of Mojidad. Early one morning he came by the pool called Narayan Dharo for bathing. Here, a sadhu, called Narayanprasad, bitterly swore and insulted Yogiji Maharaj. Yogiji Maharaj did not reply in retaliation. Instead, he smilingly bore the brunt of his hostility.

A few days later, the same sadhu was travelling in torrential rains from Botad to Sarangpur. It was late night when he reached Sarangpur and found the doors of the old mandir closed. So he knocked at the gate of the Akshar Purushottam Mandir. On seeing a sadhu, the guard opened the wicket gate and let him in.

Yogiji Maharaj was awake, sitting by the steps of the main porch. He cordially welcomed Narayanprasad and attended to his needs. Yogiji Maharaj removed a thorn from the sole of his feet, served him food and then laid a mattress for him to rest. Narayanprasad was touched by Yogiji Maharaj's service and broke down asking for forgiveness, "You are the embodiment of love because you do good even to those who have harmed you."

Despite the once unfriendly actions of Narayanprasad, Yogiji Maharaj responded with love and a spirit to alleviate his suffering. Yogiji Maharaj was truly a confluence of tolerance and love.

6. FAULT-FINDING

By seeing faults in God, Satpurush and devotees, one commits the act of fault-finding.

1. *A person who lacks wisdom, when he does satsang and listens to discourses in Satsang, continually perceives virtues within himself. Moreover, when God and His Sant highlight his flaws and advise him, he misinterprets such advice due to his arrogance. On the contrary, he perceives flaws in God and His Sant. Such a person steadily declines and loses his reputation in Satsang.*
    - Vachanāmrut Gadhadā I-6

2. *One who believes one's self to be the body and does not have an intense aversion for the panchvishays would spite a sadhu if he were to denounce the vishays, even though the sadhu may be senior. Such a person would ultimately spite God as well.*
    - Vachanāmrut Loyā-17

3. *A person who has perceived flaws in the Sant will certainly, at some time, fall from Satsang. He should be known to have his head severed.*
    - Vachanāmrut Loyā-1

4. *The best of all things is to have the association of God and this Sadhu; and there is nothing better to understand than this.*
    And what is the worst of all things? – to perceive human traits in this Sadhu.
    - Swāmini Vāto: 3.36

Story 1

Dinanath Bhatt

Mayaram Bhatt was a genuine devotee of Shriji Maharaj. As an ideal householder, Maharaj wrote his name in the Shikshapatri. This did not suit Dinanath Bhatt who was a great pundit from Amod. Though Dinanath revered Shriji Maharaj, he became critical towards Maharaj because of his jealousy for Mayaram.

The consequences of Dinanath's blasphemy took its toll on his daughter. She became possessed by a terrible ghost. Dinanath sought all possible ways and means to exorcise the ghost, but failed.

Finally, he went to Shriji Maharaj who was in Gadhada. There, he repented and begged forgiveness for his sins. The all-compassionate Maharaj blessed him and said, "Go to Mayaram Bhatt, he shall exorcise the ghost."

Dinanath obeyed and asked Mayaram to help him. Mayaram prayed to Maharaj, took some water and sprinkled it on Dinanath's daughter. In an instant the ghost fled and Dinanath's daughter began to behave normally.

By perceiving faults in a genuine devotee of God, one invites pain and misery. Even God becomes helpless to redeem a sinner who bears ill will towards His devotee.

Story 2

"Gone, Gone and Gone..."

Gunatitanand Swami's enlightening discourses attracted a large multitude of devotees from Gujarat, Sorath and Kathiawad. In his divine presence sins dissolved, pressures of life eased and the soul became enriched with the glory of Shriji Maharaj.

Two devotees from Pij arrived in Junagadh to listen to

Swami's discourses. On entering the mandir, they encountered a double-thumbed sadhu. The sadhu was averse to Gunatitanand Swami. He tried to stall both the devotees, but one of them walked off, while the other got ensnared in his sweet hospitality. The former devotee went to the assembly hall and prostrated before Gunatitanand Swami. Swami called him near, asked him how he was and then enquired about his companion. The devotee was amazed at Swami's omniscient powers and replied, "He has stayed behind over there and said he'll come soon."

At this Gunatitanand Swami responded, "He has gone, gone and gone!"

The devotee did not understand Swami's statement but Jaga Swami enquired, "Swami can you explain your words."

"He will no longer be able to take refuge of the *Satpurush*. His soul will regress from Satsang due to words of hatred and ill will instilled by that sadhu. For him the path of redemption has closed. His soul will be consigned to the miseries of hell and the cycle of births and deaths." And so saying, Gunatitanand Swami remained silent.

The holy Sadhu is the means to redemption. By nourishing enmity towards him one closes the path to *moksha*. A true aspirant avoids blasphemous talks and never even thinks of it.

Story 3

"One-way!"

In 1960, Yogiji Maharaj was on a *satsang* tour of Zambia. On 31 March he left Lusaka for Brokenhill. On the way they came across a barrier of barrels and a signboard saying, "Road closed ahead." Rajnibhai, the driver, removed the barrels and drove ahead.

When Yogiji Maharaj enquired why he was going ahead despite the signboard, Rajnibhai replied, "Bapa! Many times the roads in Africa are functioning and still one finds such signboards." Swamishri remained quiet. After a while they arrived at a point where the road was broken. There was no way they could turn around because the road was narrow and high above ground level. The only option left was to reverse the car all the way back. When Rajnibhai reversed his car, Yogiji Maharaj grasped the situation. He raised his hand and said, "One-way! Roads closed. Likewise, Akshardham is also one-way. For one who sees another's faults the roads are closed. One should never engage oneself in fault-finding. Always see and tread the path of virtue."

Yogiji Maharaj plainly but effectively conveyed that by seeing another's faults one regresses.

Yogiji Maharaj often said, "For 50 years I have been in *Satsang*. Never in any devotee – however ordinary or incapable he may be – have I taken his faults. Whatever his nature, even if he is hostile to me, I have not felt ill-will for him."

Not seeing another's faults is a fundamental propagated by the holy Sadhu. To see and harp upon another's faults are like taking poison. A true devotee never looks at another's faults.

7. HUMILITY

Discarding one's ego and behaving with servitude and respect towards God, the Satpurush and His devotees is known as *nirmanipanu* (humility).

1. *The enjoyment which one experiences from vanity cannot be obtained from any other object. Thus, amongst all devotees, a person who forsakes vanity and worships God should be known to be an extremely great devotee.*
   - Vachanāmrut Gadhadā II-41

2. *It is not appropriate to be conceited before God or His Sant. Before them, putting conceit aside, behaving as a servant of servants and becoming humble is the only appropriate behaviour.*
   - Vachanāmrut Panchālā-5

3. *A person who remains arrogant due to the vanity of his gnān, vairāgya and bhakti may be called great, but his greatness will be very limited; he does not imbibe the great virtues imbibed by a humble devotee.*
   - Vachanāmrut Gadhadā I-56

4. *Dāsnā dās thaine, vali je rahe Satsangmā;*
   Bhakti teni bhali mānish, rāchish tenā sangmā
   - Bhaktachintāmani: 68.10

   "To one who stays in Satsang out of utter servitude, his *bhakti* I (Shriji Maharaj) shall behold as genuine and I shall enjoy his company."

5. *What is humility? To tolerate insults, attain absolute servitude, clean refuse heaps and pick up used leaf-plates.*
   - Yogiji Maharaj

6.   *Nānese ho nāne rahiye, jaisi nāni doob,*
      Ghās fis sab ood gayā, doob khoob ki khoob.

"Be smaller than the small like a blade of grass, whereas the stiff blade of grass (like an arrogant person) is rooted."

Story 1

A Satsangi of the Cot

Once, Shriji Maharaj was seated on a cot beneath a neem tree in the courtyard of Dada Khachar's darbar. Maharaj questioned the assembly of devotees, "Are you *satsangis* (followers) of this cot or the *satsangis* of *satsangis*?"

Seeing Maharaj seated on the cot, the devotees replied, "Maharaj! We are the *satsangis* of the cot."

"Then come nearer my cot," Maharaj called everyone. Within moments the whole assembly gathered around His cot.

At that moment Parvatbhai arrived and Maharaj asked him, "Are you a *satsangi* of this cot or a *satsangi* of *satsangis*?"

"Maharaj I am a *satsangi* of *satsangis*," Parvatbhai replied.

Shriji Maharaj then told him to sit afar and then went upto him and sat beside him.

The *satsangis* who were by the cot enquired, "Maharaj, why did you do this?"

"You can sit by the cot and associate with it. I am a *satsangi* of *satsangis*," Shriji Maharaj replied.

The *satsangis* understood the purpose of Maharaj's words. They realised that if we remain humble in Satsang, by becoming a devotee of devotees, then Maharaj will reside with us. Through humility, respect and service to His devotees, God and His holy Sadhu are pleased.

Story 2

One Who Serves Is Mahant

Gunatitanand Swami was once sweeping the courtyard of Junagadh mandir. On hearing the glory of the mandir and Gunatitanand Swami, the Mahant of Tarnetar mandir came with his disciples for Swami's *darshan*.

He had not met Gunatitanand Swami before, so he asked him, "Where can I meet the *mahant* of this mandir?"

Gunatitanand Swami answered while sweeping, "You can go and sit in the assembly hall. He will come there shortly."

The *mahant* and his disciples went to the assembly hall. A little while later Gunatitanand Swami, having washed his hands and feet, came and occupied the main seat and asked, "Can I help you!" The Mahant was surprised to see Gunatitanand Swami and asked, "You are the Mahant of this mandir? But you were just sweeping the courtyard!"

Gunatitanand Swami smilingly replied, "Here, one who serves humbly is the Mahant."

The noble spiritual masters reflect the ideals of greatness through their actions. Humble service is the hallmark of true greatness. One who dissolves his ego and serves Satsang is blessed by God.

Story 3

Scrubbed the Utensils

On 21 May 1950, Shastriji Maharaj was residing at Amblivali Pol in Ahmedabad. On that day, he had invited the leading devotees and senior sadhus for an historic occasion. In their presence, Shastriji Maharaj appointed Shastri Narayanswarupdas as the President of the Bochasanwasi Shri Akshar Purushottam Swaminarayan Sanstha. This milestone event was welcomed by one and all. Shastri Narayanswarupdas

prayed before Shastriji Maharaj and the devotees that he be able
to humbly serve the Sanstha till his last breath.

After the occasion, the devotees had their meals and left.
Their unwashed pile of dishes lay by the water tap. Without a
moment's hesitation, the newly appointed President, Shastri
Narayanswarupdas, sat down to scrub and wash the dishes.

He had truly understood the presidential appointment not
as a position for bossing over others, but as an opportunity to
serve humbly. Ever since, Pramukh Swami Maharaj has been
serving humbly without any distinction of high or low. He is an
embodiment of humility.

8. OBSERVANCE OF NIYAMS

Observance of *niyams* means obeying moral and spiritual commands.

1. *Whether or not one has* vairāgya, *if one diligently observes the* niyams *prescribed by God, then the desires for the* panchvishays *can be conquered.*
   - *Vachanāmrut Gadhadā II-16*

2. *One should indulge in the* vishays *only as prescribed in the scriptures; but one should never indulge in them by transgressing the regulations that are described in the scriptures.*
   - *Vachanāmrut Gadhadā I-8*

3. *If Brahmā and all the other deities follow God's commands, then how can I not follow His injunctions? Bearing this in mind, he always abides by the* niyams *prescribed by God.*
   - *Vachanāmrut Vartāl-3*

4. *Like a village that has a fort, life too has forts in the form of five-cardinal vows. And in that, like the sentry point, we have* niyams. *Just as the sentry point protects the fort, the* niyams *protect the vows. So know the laxity in* niyams *as breaches in life.*
   - *Swāmini Vāto: 5.100*

5. *The bonds of* dharma *do not bind, but are the means to liberation.*
   - *Pramukh Swami Maharaj*

Story 1

Shining Character

Sagram Vaghri of Limli village was a genuine devotee of Shriji Maharaj. Though he was low-born, by character he was noble and towering. The severe famine of VS 1869 (1813 CE) had spread its tentacles of suffering and death on the land of Kathiawad. Many migrated to southern Gujarat to survive and eke out a livelihood.

Sagram Vaghri and his wife, too, were heading optimistically towards the town of Surat. On the way Sagram's eyes fell on a shiny ornament. It was an expensive silver anklet that someone had lost. Despite his poverty, Sagram had no desire to take it. But he thought of his wife who was a few furlongs behind him. Being a woman she would be enticed to take it, and it would amount to a transgression of Bhagwan Swaminarayan's words. So thinking, Sagram covered the anklet with mud.

After a while when his wife caught up with him, she asked, "What were you doing sitting down a little while back?" Sagram revealed to her about the silver anklet and added, "To prevent you from seeing it, I covered it with mud."

"Why did you cover mud upon mud? I see another's possession as mud!" Sagram's wife nobly responded. Sagram was surprised and fascinated by his wife's resolve.

Even in spite of hard times, Sagram remained steadfast to Bhagwan Swaminarayan's instruction of not taking a thing lying on the wayside. And his wife perceived another's belonging as mud!

The strength of one's character is reflected in hard times.

9. GLORY OF SADHU

Realising the glory and knowledge of a God-realised Sadhu is the essence of *satsang*.

1. *A Sant with such a conviction is so highly respected by Me that even I place the dust of his feet on My head. In My mind, I am afraid of harming him, and I also long to have his darshan.*

   - Vachanāmrut Gadhadā I-37

2. *By seeking the refuge of the Satpurush, regardless of how terrible a sinner a person may be, he becomes extremely pure.*

   - Vachanāmrut Vartāl-14

3. *If a person develops conviction in the guru – who is the manifest form of God – in the same way that he has conviction in the non-manifest demigods, then, as a result, he attains all of the arthas* which are described as attainable.*

   - Vachanāmrut Gadhadā III-2

4. *What are the characteristics of a Sant who is worthy of being worshipped on par with God? Well, such a Sant suppresses the actions of māyā's gunas – the indriyas, the antahkaran, etc.; but he himself does not get suppressed by their actions. In addition to this, he only performs activities related to God; he is staunch in his observance of the five religious vows; and believing himself to be brahmarup, he worships Purushottam Bhagwan. Such a Sant should not be thought of as a human being, nor should he be thought of as a demigod, because such behaviour is not possible for either humans or deities.*

   - Vachanāmrut Gadhadā III-26

---

*Here 'arthas' should be understood as 'purushārths' – *dharma, artha, kām* and *moksha*.

Story 1

Glory of the Satpurush

Once, Shastriji Maharaj was in Anand. Before him were devotees who had profound glory and commitment to the Akshar Purushottam creed. Shastriji Maharaj asked Manibhai, "What is the glory of the Satpurush?" Manibhai was well acquainted with the Sampraday's scriptures and thus answered with references from the Vachanamrut.

Shastriji Maharaj acknowledged what he said and added, "Say there is a dense jungle similar to the forests of Africa, where even the rays of the afternoon sun cannot penetrate. And this jungle is full of wild animals. If someone were to go there and loudly proclaim the name 'Bhagatji', then any living thing that hears this name will be redeemed. This is the glory of the Satpurush."

The mere remembrance of the bona fide sadhu or Satpurush can dissolve evil tendencies in one's soul. Even through his direct or indirect communion, the soul is redeemed.

Story 2

64 Holy Places

The Annakut festival in Junagadh had been gloriously celebrated. Pragji Bhagat was an idol of service. He had resolved to scrub and wash all the utensils used for the Annakut festival. While he was scouring the pots and pans, Gunatitanand Swami came to him. The flow of clean water touched Swami's feet and fell into a trough. Gunatitanand Swami asked Pragji Bhagat, "Where are the 64 holy places?"

"At the holy feet of the Satpurush!" replied Pragji Bhagat.

Swami then smiled and tellingly said, "If one understands this, then one will be redeemed."

Pragji Bhagat, out of his profuse reverence for Swami, jumped into the dirty water to sanctify himself. To others it seemed that he had dirtied himself but in fact he was bathing in nectar.

Story 3

"Believe the Satpurush
to Be My Form..."

Sadguru Nishkulanand Swami, a leading *paramhansa* of Bhagwan Swaminarayan, has profusely written poetry and lyrics that reflect the spirit of renunciation, detachment, morality and the glory of *bhakti*.

In all his works, he has predominantly focussed on the glory of the Gunatit Satpurush. He sung them with enthusiasm and absolute clarity. A few examples of his literary creations are as follows:

1. *Kāmdughā kalpataru, pāras chintāmani chār,*
   Sant samān eke nahi, me manmā karyo vichār.

- Bhaktachintāmani: 2/7

I have thought that out of four wish-fulfilling things, namely, the cow, tree, philosopher's stone and gem; none are equal to the Satpurush.

2. *Santkrupāe sukh upaje santkrupāthi sare kām,*
   Santkrupāthi pāmiye puran Purushottam dhām.

- Bhaktachintāmani: 2/2

Through the grace of the Sant one attains happiness, through his grace one accomplishes works and through his grace one attains the absolute abode of Purushottam.

3. *Sant hu ne hu to vali Sant re,*
    Em Shrimukhe kahe Bhagwant re,
    Sant mānajo māri murti re,
    Emā fera nathi ek rati re

                                    - Nishkulānand Kāvya:
                                    Purushottam Prakāsh, 41/9

Referring to what Bhagwan Swaminarayan said
Nishkulanand Swami explains, "The Sant is Me and I am
the Sant. Believe the Sant to be My form and there is not an
iota of difference between us."

4. *Ke'she sant to a bahu sārā re,*
    Kharā kalyānnā karnārā re,
    Etalo ja guna koi gre'she re,
    Te to Brahmamahole vās leshe re.

                                    - Nishkulānand Kāvya:
                                    Purushottam Prakāsh, 41/14

If anyone says that this Sant is very good and the true
redeemer; by appreciating this virtue he will attain
Brahmamahol (highest abode of God).

5. *Sant desh pardesh fare chhe re,*
    Sahu jivanā agh hare chhe re,
    Enā darshan, sparsh je karshe re,
    Te to Bhavajal pār utarshe re.

                                    - Nishkulānand Kāvya:
                                    Purushottam Prakāsh, 41/19

The bona fide Sant travels to relieve the sins of all souls.
Whosoever has his *darshan* and touches him will be redeemed from the ocean of life.

6. *Dhanya dhanya e Sant sujan ne,*
    Jenu ulati palatyu āp... Sant te swayam Hari.
    Āp tali malyā Bhagwanmā,
    Jenā āpmā Harino vyāp ...Sant te swayam Hari.

                                    - Nishkulānand Swami

Glorious is the Sant whose inner self is not mundane ... (for)
he is God Himself.
You have lost yourself and become one with God.
In you pervades God... hence, he is God Himself.

10. REFUGE

Ashro, or refuge, is surrendering to God and believing Him to be the giver of happiness and ultimate redemption.

1. *One who has such a firm refuge of God, even if he were to experience pain equivalent to that of final dissolution, he would not believe anyone else to be his guardian against such misery except God. Moreover, whatever happiness he wishes for, he seeks to attain only from God. That is, he does not consider anyone but God to be the source of happiness. Moreover, he behaves only according to the wishes of God. Such a person can be known to have taken refuge in God. It is he who can be called a staunch devotee of God.*

   - Vachanāmrut Vartāl-5

2. *Accepting the firm refuge of God is the single, greatest endeavour amongst all spiritual endeavours for pleasing God. That refuge, though, must be extremely firm and without any flaws.*

   - Vachanāmrut Gadhadā I-33

3. *When God is not manifest on this earth, one should seek the refuge of the Sant who has the realisation of God – because the* jiva *can also attain liberation through him.*

   - Vachanāmrut Vartāl-10

4. *No matter how sinful or insignificant a person may be, if he seeks the refuge of God and His Bhakta, that person will become absolutely fulfilled.*

   - Vachanāmrut Gadhadā II-62

5. *If terrible obstacles are in store then they will be dissolved with refuge in God and the great Sadhu. Otherwise, no matter how much one may endeavour till death, still they will not be solved.*

   - Swāmini Vāto: 1.114

Story 1

Liberation in Refuge

Shriji Maharaj and the *paramhansas* were present in Gadhada. Once, Maharaj instructed the *paramhansas*, "From today onwards you shall all wear an arm's length of jute cloth only." Then Maharaj started giving the jute cloth to the *paramhansas*. Everyone present accepted the new injunction.

Then Brahmanand Swami came. Since he was very fat, an arm's length of jute cloth did not suffice for him.

"Maharaj, give me more than an arm's length," Brahmanand Swami requested.

"A rule is a rule. You'll not get more," Maharaj replied.

"But Maharaj, how can I cover myself with only an arm's length!" Brahmanand Swami argued.

"Then reduce your weight. I will not give you an inch more."

On hearing this, Brahmanand Swami started looking in the four directions. Shriji Maharaj asked him what he was doing.

"I am looking around to see whether there is any God besides You residing anywhere. But I cannot find anyone other than You. Without refuge in You there is no liberation," Brahmanand Swami spoke with deep conviction and reverence for Maharaj.

The words of Brahmanand Swami pleased Maharaj. The supreme Maharaj embraced and showered His blessings on Brahmanand Swami and gave him the extra jute cloth. Everyone was impressed by the resolute faith of Brahmanand Swami.

A devotee's firm refuge in God makes him a recipient of liberation and God's abundant grace.

Story 2

Naja Jogiya of Bhoyra

Naja Bhakta was a devotee of Shriji Maharaj who lived in the village of Bhoyra. The village king was called Vasur Khachar. He was very cruel and harsh on criminals. Even for petty crimes he subjected them to inhuman torture and had their knees broken.

Once, Vasur Khachar called Naja Jogiya and asked him, "Is your Swaminarayan really God?

"Yes," replied the pious Naja.

"Then let Him come here tomorrow morning to give me *darshan*. And if He doesn't arrive by morning, then I shall break your knees!" roared the ruthless Vasur Khachar.

Naja Jogiya was a dedicated and faithful devotee. He had no other refuge than Maharaj Himself. So he prayed all night to Him to come and transform the evil king.

At that time Shriji Maharaj was in Visnagar. The all-knowing Maharaj heard the prayers of His devotee, and thus left for Bhoyra immediately. He walked barefoot all night, crossed the river Bhogavo and reached Bhoyra at the break of dawn. Naja Jogiya was overwhelmed by Maharaj's *darshan*. He went to the king's court and with one divine glance sent him into a *samadhi* where he experienced the hellish punishments for his sins. After awakening from the *samadhi* the king asked for forgiveness and pledged to live righteously.

One who has firm faith in God is protected by Him from obstacles and misery. The attribute of a true devotee is to have resolute faith in God.

Story 3

Swaminarayan – the Guardian
and Protector

Barpatoli is a small village in Saurashtra. Khima Dobariya, a native of the village, was a dedicated devotee of Bhagwan Swaminarayan. He was happy socially and financially. He had a respectable name in the region. His wife, too, was a staunch devotee.

One afternoon, an astrologer came to Khima Dobariya's house. Though by appearance he donned a pair of odd clothes and sported a heavy beard, Khima Dobariya's wife welcomed him thinking that he was a Brahmin. After a while he turned the pages of a voluminous book and uttered, "Lady, I am warning you with reference to the scriptures of astrology that your husband's stars have now become unfavourable."

"What do you mean by unfavourable?" Khima's wife enquired. And the Brahmin took the opportunity to prey upon the woman's apparent gullibility. He uttered a chain of references and stories and added, "It means that he will have to beg for alms from village to village and will go hungry for days on end."

At this, Khima's wife responded emphatically, "There are no unfavourable stars shining on my husband's fate. He has happily had his lunch and is now peacefully taking an afternoon nap on his farm. So it seems that it is not his stars but yours that are unfavourable. Otherwise why would you have to come roaming all the way from Gujarat to Kathiawad to earn your living!"

The Brahmin was simply astonished at the unexpected answer. Then Khima Dobariya's wife added, "Listen, O stranger! We have Swaminarayan as our guardian and protector. Through His powers no amount of mumbo-jumbo or black magic can affect us."

The Brahmin left in shame, never to return to that village.

A true devotee has unswerving faith in God. He does not believe in black magic nor can evil elements exercise their influence over him or her.

11. FAITH

Faith is having absolute trust in God and the Satpurush's words and actions and in the words of the scriptures.

1. *If you keep firm faith in Me and do as I say, then even if you were to suffer extreme hardships, or even if you were to face the calamities of seven consecutive famines, I will protect you from them. Even if you were made to suffer miseries from which there seems to be no way out, I will still protect you.*

   - Vachanāmrut Jetalpur-5

2. *Only one who has faith in the scriptures is able to develop unshakeable faith in God, and only such a person attains liberation. In addition, such a person would never deviate from dharma.*

   - Vachanāmrut Sārangpur-13

3. *Moreover, a person who does not trust a draft signed by a wealthy businessman should be known to be a fool – because he does not realise the wealth of that businessman. Similarly, one who does not trust the words of greats such as Nārad, Sanakādik, Vyās, Vālmiki, etc., should be known as a* nāstik *and a grave sinner.*

   - Vachanāmrut Gadhadā II-6

4. *Only the one who possesses faith is better. Rāmchandraji has said in the Rāmāyan, 'I protect one who has firm faith in me – just as a mother protects her child.' Therefore, only the one with faith is better.*

   - Vachanāmrut Gadhadā III-14

Story 1

First Step in Satsang

Krupanand Swami was a great *paramhansa* of Shriji Maharaj. Gunatitanand Swami had stayed for many years under Krupanand Swami. Once Krupanand Swami's group was travelling at the foot of Mt. Girnar. The mountain was a retreat for many yogis and sadhus engaged in various spiritual endeavours. One such sannyasi was circumambulating Mt. Girnar through prostrations. When Gunatitanand Swami saw the sannyasi he asked him why he was prostrating. The sannyasi replied, "Because if there is a great realised sadhu on Girnar, then my single prostration will bless me with *moksha*."

Gunatitanand Swami was amazed at his incredible faith. He told the sannyasi, "Our Krupanand Swami is a great sadhu. If you prostrate to him, you will be redeemed."

But the sannyasi did not believe Swami's words. And what's more, he had already decided his own path of spiritual endeavours. Therefore, he failed to understand the glory of Krupanand Swami.

The sannyasi replied, "If he comes on my path then I shall prostrate before him." And so saying, he proceeded prostrating on his fixed path.

Gunatitanand Swami felt pity for the soul's poverty. Faith in the words of a Gunatit Sadhu is the first and most important step in Satsang. Without faith one's endeavours are like a tree without fruits.

Story 2

The Power of Faith

Vagha Khachar of Sarangpur was a dedicated and coura- geous devotee. Once, Gunatitanand Swami stopped by at Sarangpur while he was on his way to Junagadh. Vagha Khachar expressed his frustration before Gunatitanand Swami, "I am being hassled by my own base nature. I still have violent dreams. On dreaming about bloodshed and killing, I wake up sweating and trembling with fear. Tell me when shall my base nature be eradicated?"

Gunatitanand Swami consoled Vagha Khachar and told him to come with him to Junagadh. Since Vagha Khachar was a senior and prominent devotee, Swami instructed Pragji Bhakta to serve him as his attendant. On the way Pragji Bhakta talked about the glory of Gunatitanand Swami. "He is Mul Akshar," Pragji Bhakta explained. But Vagha Khachar did not believe that Swami was Mul Akshar, so he was annoyed and scolded the latter severely. When they reached Junagadh, Vagha Khachar saw the joy on the faces of the devotees of Sorath. He enquired as to why they were so happy.

"Because we have understood the glory of Gunatitanand Swami. If you want to experience divine joy, then you, too, should believe Swami is Mul Akshar," the devotees revealed.

"If Swami tells me himself, then I shall believe him," proposed Vagha Khachar.

On meeting Gunatitanand Swami, Vagha Khachar asked, "Everyone believes you to be Mul Akshar. Is this true?"

"Yes, I am Mul Akshar," replied Swami.

On hearing it from Swami's mouth, Vagha Khachar was convinced. He had faith in Swami and his conviction in Swami's greatness as Mul Akshar opened the doorway to divine joy. Vagha Khachar became blessed with the power to see Shriji Maharaj. From that moment onwards his inner weaknesses of ego, anger, lust, etc. vanished.

Faith is the spiritual elixir that redeems the soul from base instincts and elevates it to the state of *brahmarup*. Faith in God or His holy Sadhu is the panacea for the sufferings from the cycle of births and deaths.

Story 3

Faith in Spiritual Words

Balmukund Swami was a blessed disciple of Gunatitanand Swami. Once, he and several sadhus arrived at a mandir in a village. During the morning discourse they read from the "Swamini Vato" of Gunatitanand Swami, "Whoever remembers God, I give unto him food to eat." Some of the *sadhus* doubted the truth of the Swamini Vatu and told Balmukund Swami, "Today, let us see whether this discourse is true or not!"

Balmukund Swami had absolute faith in the sermons of Gunatitanand Swami. He told all the sadhus to remember Maharaj and sing His glory. More than three hours elapsed and it was nearly 12 noon. No one, till then, had approached them with offerings of food. Many of the sadhus felt that they would have to cook food for Thakorji.

But at the stroke of 12 noon, a devotee came to the mandir. He was followed by several people carrying some baskets. The devotee bowed before the sadhus and said, "Swami, I was on my way to my son's wedding. When I came to the outskirts of this village, I was pleased to hear that you and several sadhus were in the mandir. I have come to offer some sweetmeats and food for Thakorji and the sadhus. Please offer it to Thakorji and bless us all..."

The sadhus were amazed to hear the devotee's words and were impressed by Balmukund Swami's faith in Gunatitanand Swami's sermons.

One who has absolute faith in God is always taken care of by God. Faith is a unique attribute of one who has a firm refuge in God. And to have such faith is a quality of a true devotee.

12. DIVINE ATTITUDE

Having divinity (*divyabhav*) towards God and His Sadhu means to believe them to be divine and devoid of all human attributes.

1. *A devotee realises, 'God is God. There is no scope for dividing or discarding any part of Him. That very God is the Atma of countless* brahmānds.' *One who has no doubts at all regarding the nature of God should be known to have attained the nirvikalp state. One with such stable understanding should be known as 'sthitapragna.'* *
   - *Vachanāmrut Gadhadā II-17*

2. *The means of acquiring such virtuous qualities is as follows: Whoever believes the great Purush to be absolutely free of flaws becomes totally flawless himself. If, however, a person perceives flaws in the great Purush, that person's intellect becomes polluted, and enemies – i.e., lust, anger, etc. – all come to dwell within his heart.*
   - *Vachanāmrut Gadhadā I-73*

3. *All of My divine actions and incidents, as well as the chanting of My name, are redemptive.*
   - *Vachanāmrut Gadhadā II-35*

4. *The Bhakta of God is indeed nothing but a form of Brahma. That is why one should never perceive human traits in him.*
   - *Vachanāmrut Gadhadā II-63*

5. *When divine feelings and human feelings become one, then one enjoys devotion to God.*
   - *Swāmini Vāto: 5.101*

---

* Literally, 'sthitapragna' means 'one with a stable mind' but here Shriji Maharaj gives His own, unique definition.

6. *The same God who is in Akshardham has come here (on earth) and He does not have the human traits of childhood, youth and old age and He never dies. However, the human traits we see are like the illusions of a magician.*

- Swāmini Vāto: 5.66

Story 1

Served the Devotees in Agatrai

Parvatbhai, of village Agatrai, was a great devotee of Bhagwan Swaminarayan. Once, Shriji Maharaj went to his village with a group of Kathi devotees. Parvatbhai rejoiced at their arrival and made everything available for their hospitality. The Kathi devotees were amazed at his generosity and spirit of respect for all of them.

One day, Parvatbhai had a sweet item made of wheat flour, sugar and ghee arranged for lunch. He then requested Maharaj to serve extra helpings of ghee on top of the servings of *kansar*. And the Supreme God, Shriji Maharaj, agreed to fulfil the desire of Parvatbhai. Maharaj started pouring ghee without interrupting its flow from one plate to the next. In spite of the ghee falling outside the plate, Parvatbhai danced joyously in circles and exclaimed, "Oh! Look at my Lord's divine *lila*. How can one get someone like Him to serve ghee in this fashion!"

On seeing Parvatbhai's divine feelings for Shriji Maharaj, everyone realised his absolute devotion for Maharaj.

Every action of God is divine. Through His divine actions, God bestows the divine joy of His *murti* to His devotees.

Story 2

"Vataldi Rahone Rataldi..."

Two ordinary brothers of Kanetar village, Sagram Vaghri and Shardul, had given up their immoral ways to become devotees of Bhagwan Swaminarayan. Sagram lived in abject poverty. He had a mud hut for his house. Once, Shriji Maharaj came to this poor devotee's doorstep without any prior message. Sagram danced with joy on seeing Maharaj.

"Sagram, hide me quickly. There is a Kathi devotee and a sadhu who are looking for Me. If they find Me here, they will surely take Me back," Maharaj said hurriedly.

Sagram was momentarily stunned because he had no idea where to hide Maharaj in his small mud hut. So he took Maharaj to his brother, Shardul's house, next door. There, pointing to a large earthen vessel, Sagram told Maharaj to get inside.

After a while Brahmanand Swami and Sura Khachar came to Sagram's hut. They cleverly questioned Sagram about Maharaj's whereabouts. During this time, Maharaj asked Sagram's wife for her clothes and put them on, so that no one would recognise Him.

But Brahmanand Swami had a strong feeling of Maharaj's presence, so he first checked Sagram's house and then told Shardul to tell all his members to come out. When Maharaj came out, donned in a woman's clothes, along with Shardul and Sagram's wives, Sura Khachar immediately recognised Shriji Maharaj's walk. Brahmanand Swami understood the situation within seconds.

"Who is the husband of that last woman!" enquired Sura Khachar.

"She is not married," Sagram replied.

On hearing Sagram's answer, Maharaj broke into a muffled laughter. Brahmanand Swami was quick to recognise it as Maharaj's laughter. And so despite Maharaj's disguise and human action, Brahmanand Swami saw Him in all divinity. His heart burst out into a song,

> Vātaldi   rahone   rātaldi
> Vālā   puchhu   ek   vātaldi

"If you stay for the night, then dear one let me ask you a question."

Story 3

Absolute Divinity

Once Pramukh Swami Maharaj was asked, "You have immensely served Shastriji Maharaj and enjoyed his *darshan*. Out of all your experiences with him which one did you find to be divine?"

Without a moment's delay Swamishri replied, "All of them. All the actions of Shastriji Maharaj were divine."

Swamishri's answer reflects the absolute divinity he perceived in his guru. For him all his actions were divine.

Perceiving divinity is the immortalising and redemptory ingredient on the path of spirituality. Swamishri often reiterates that, "Whatever faults or discrepancies we see in the holy Sadhu is a reflection of our own faults and base nature. He is absolutely pure. The more one consolidates a divine perspective (*divyabhav*) towards him, the happier one becomes."

13. ABSOLUTE FAITH

Absolute faith or conviction in one's mind is *nishchay*. God and His Sadhu are the truth. God is supreme, there is nothing or nobody greater than Him. This firm belief is absolute faith.

1. One possessing the highest level of 'nirvikalp faith' realises that countless millions of brahmānds, each encircled by the eight barriers, appear like mere atoms before Akshar. Such is the greatness of Akshar, the abode of Purushottam Nārāyan. One who worships Purushottam having become aksharrup can be said to possess the highest level of 'nirvikalp faith'.

   - Vachanāmrut Loyā-12

2. The attributes of the Sant – being free of lust, avarice, egotism, taste, attachment, etc. – are also described in the scriptures. The Sant who possesses these attributes has a direct relationship with God. Therefore, one should develop the conviction of God based on his words. In fact, to have firm faith in the words of the Sant is itself the conviction of God.

   - Vachanāmrut Gadhadā III-27

3. What would a person who has faith in God and His Sant coupled with the knowledge of their greatness not do for the sake of God and His Sant? For them, he would renounce his family, renounce any fear of public ridicule, renounce a kingdom, renounce pleasures, renounce wealth, renounce his wife, and in the case of a woman, she would renounce her husband.

   - Vachanāmrut Loyā-3

4. One who has the firm conviction of God – i.e., who has realised God completely by believing that there are no māyik qualities in His form and that that God transcends māyā and the products of māyā, the three gunas – has transcended God's māyā.

   - Vachanāmrut Vartāl-5

5. *If a person realises this greatness of Purushottam Bhagwān
   by profound association with the Sant, then all of his*
   indriyas *and* antahkarans *become divine like Purushottam
   Bhagwān's* indriyas *and* antahkaran. *Then, through those*
   indriyas *and* antahkarans, *he can develop the conviction of
   that God.*

   - Vachanāmrut Gadhadā I-51

6. *The characteristics of one who has* nishchay *in God and His
   Ekāntik Sadhu are: just as a person who has 1000 million*
   maunds *of grain and plenty of money has no fear of death
   from famine; and just as one who is protected by 2000
   guards does not fear being robbed, similarly, one who has*
   nishchay *has no fear of* kāl, karma *or* māyā. *He believes
   himself to be fulfilled and has no desires except for that of
   God.*

   - Swāmini Vāto: 5.2

Story 1

Nityanand Swami's Faith

Shriji Maharaj tested his *paramhansas* in many ways, yet
their conviction in His divinity never faltered.

From time-to-time Maharaj would engage in some *lila* and
give the *paramhansas* some divine memories to cherish.

Once, during an assembly Shriji Maharaj asked Nityanand
Swami, "How firm is your faith?"

Realising this as an opportunity to hail the glory of Shriji
Maharaj, Nityanand Swami declared, "Maharaj! At present You
have a large group of sadhus and devotees. Your glory and
greatness is spreading everywhere. However, even if You had
none of this, and were married with five to seven children and
so poor that You had insufficient food to eat and as a result were
begging in the Mandvi Bazaar of Vadodara, my faith that You
are the supreme God would never waver."

Maharaj was pleased with Nityanand Swami's firm faith and

said, "Yes, Swami! You really do possess firm faith." With this Maharaj affectionately embraced Nityanand Swami.

A true devotee of God sees total divinity in every action of God. A true devotee with the highest faith firmly believes, "God is God. His form is totally divine."

Story 2

Himraj Sheth of Sundariyana

Himraj Sheth and his sons, residents of Sundariyana, near Botad, were attracted into Satsang through Gopalanand Swami. Himraj Sheth and his sons had an unshakeable faith that Shriji Maharaj was the supreme God.

Due to their change of allegiance from the Vaishnav Sampraday to the Swaminarayan Sampraday, many people of their community caused them much trouble. However, they were determined to adhere to their new-found faith, whatever the consequences.

After some time, Himraj Sheth passed away. So, people attempted to convince his sons, Vanasha and Pujasha, to forsake Satsang and throw away their *kanthi*. The community leaders decided that they would attend Himraj Sheth's final rites only if the sons gave up Satsang.

Despite this threat, the sons were resolute that they would never give up Satsang and their firm faith towards Maharaj. As a final measure, the community leaders excommunicated Himraj Sheth's sons from their community.

When Shriji Maharaj learnt of this, He immediately arrived in Sundariyana with a large entourage of sadhus and devotees to attend Himraj Sheth's final rites. Vanasha and Pujasha were overjoyed.

Maharaj, too, gave everyone immense spiritual bliss through His discourses, *darshan* and *prasad*.

A devotee with true faith remains unshaken even in the face of stiffest opposition. God always protects those who have such firm faith.

Story 3

Vajiba of Vijapur

Vajiba, one of Maharaj's foremost female devotees, was of the Sathvara community. She lived in Vijapur and readily and devoutly served food and provided clothes for all sadhus. Once, she had understood the qualities of a true sadhu and the principles of Satsang, she became a very staunch devotee. She realised the futility of feeding and clothing wayward *bawas* and thus stopped entertaining them.

Once, Shriji Maharaj arrived with Mulji Brahmachari to Vajiba's house. As she had never seen Shriji Maharaj, she did not recognise Him. Maharaj tested the extent of her faith by showing several miracles. Through His powers of omniscience, He asked for *rotlas*, a bed and a mattress. Even when He extended His feet to touch a pipal tree, she did not waver in her faith towards Maharaj. In fact, her firmness increased, even though she did not know that Maharaj Himself was her visitor.

A few days after Maharaj had left, she decided to go to Gadhada for His *darshan*. There, Maharaj asked her, "Do you recognise these *charnarvind?*

Vajiba replied, "Maharaj! This is the first time I am having your *darshan*."

Maharaj said, "These are the feet that stretched out to touch your pipal tree."

Surprised, Vajiba responded, "Oh Maharaj! Was it You who came that day? I didn't even recognise You. And I treated You very harshly."

Maharaj smiled as He listened and then comforting Vajiba, said, "I had come to test you. Your faith did not waver in the slightest. Even if devotees like you treat Me harshly, I find it very soothing!"

Devotees who have firm faith are not deflected from their conviction, even if tested by God Himself. God showers His love on such staunch devotees.

14. PAKSH

To side totally – through mind, action and words – with God and His devotee. To be partisan or supportive towards them is *paksh*.

1. *In no way should one abandon one's loyalty to God and His Bhakta, even if while keeping that loyalty one's reputation increases or decreases, or one is honoured or insulted, or one lives or dies.*

   - Vachanāmrut Gadhadā III-7

2. *Consider a woman who observes the vow of fidelity. Even if her husband is old, sick, poor or ugly, the mind of that faithful wife would never swerve upon seeing the virtues of another man. Even if a beggar's wife, who observes such a vow, were to see a great king, her mind would not waver.... One who does side with a non-believer will himself, either in this life or in the next, definitely become a non-believer as well. Therefore, a devotee of God should certainly side with God's devotees and forsake the side of non-believers.*

   - Vachanāmrut Gadhadā II-5

3. *One should be absolutely loyal to a devotee of God – just as one is loyal to one's relatives and one's mother and father.*

   - Vachanāmrut Gadhadā II-60

4. *Just as one is loyal to one's relatives, if a person is similarly loyal to Satsang, then his foundation in Satsang is firm.*

   - Vachanāmrut Gadhadā I-78

Story 1

The Ultimate Sacrifice

Once, a group of Shriji Maharaj's sadhus arrived in the village of Gundali. Two brothers, named Meraman and Mamaiya lived there. Their mother was a devout *satsangi*. Hearing the news of the sadhus' arrival, she requested a devotee to invite them to her house. When they came, she provided them the necessary items to cook their meal.

The son of the village chieftain was totally opposed to Satsang. When he learnt that the sadhus of Swaminarayan had come, he quickly took a group of his accomplices to Mamaiya's house. There, they threw away the food the sadhus had cooked, beat them severely and drove them out of the village.

Meraman and Mamaiya arrived home from the farm at lunch-time. They saw their mother crying and asked her what had happened. "The son of the village chief beat our sadhus and drove them out of the village," she explained. Hearing this, the brothers were enraged. They sent their mother off to Gadhada and made their way to the chief's home. There, the chief's son was seated with a group of his friends. In an instant, the brothers threw a dagger and the chief's son dropped dead. Then the brothers mounted their horses and rode off speedily.

The village chief immediately sent his troops after them. In the ensuing fight, both brothers were killed.

When Shriji Maharaj heard this news, He said, "Those who side with the sadhus in this way deserve praise. They died supporting My sadhus, so I give them Akshardham in return."

One should not hesitate to support a devotee of God, even at the cost of one's life.

Story 2

"Gift of Akshardham."

There was commotion in the court of Vajesinh Bapu, the king of Bhavnagar. The reason: Mulu Charan of Tatana had become drunk and was hurling abuse at the good name of Bhagwan Swaminarayan.

Of those present, some found his outburst entertaining, while some observed indifference and listened silently. Then, Mulu Charan's abuse became more venomous.

In the court, a devotee named Narsinh Joshi was present. His hair stood on end as he heard this uncalled for tirade. Shedding his timidity, he challenged Mulu Charan. Mulu Charan was stunned by this. Narsinh Joshi upheld the good name of Bhagwan Swaminarayan and pointed out his mistake. As the truth came out, Charan's false accusations were disproved. In the end, Narsinh Joshi spoke sternly to Charan to stop him from blaspheming Bhagwan Swaminarayan ever again. All those present realised that Mulu Charan's accusations were false and they began to ridicule him.

Thus, Narsinh Joshi upheld the name of Bhagwan Swaminarayan. When Maharaj heard of this, He showered His blessings upon him for his allegiance, saying, "Joshi! You stood up for Me. So in return I bestow upon you the gift of Akshardham."

So Joshi's support (*paksh*) earned him Akshardham.

Such support is a characteristic of a devotee with undivided faith.

Story 3

Jinabhai's Selfless Service

Jinabhai of Panchala was a staunch devotee of Shriji Maharaj. Once, he went from Mangrol to Loj for some work. There, he learnt that a devotee named Kamalshibhai Vanza had fallen very ill. The news caused Jinabhai much concern, so he decided to bring Kamalshibhai to Panchala for treatment. Kamalshibhai was also very touched by Jinabhai's care.

One day, Kamalshibhai had a severe headache. So, Jinabhai asked his sister, Adiba, for some black pepper. But Adiba, who was not too pleased at having Kamalshibhai at home, refused, saying that there was none left – even though there was some in stock.

A few days later, Jinabhai had a headache, and this time Adiba immediately gave him some black pepper to relieve his pain.

Jinabhai realised what Adiba had done and scolded her, saying, "You refused the black pepper for Kamalshibhai, whereas today you bring it for me without any hesitation". With this, he threw it away and stopped speaking to his sister.

This was the extent of attachment and support Jinabhai had for the devotees of Maharaj. That is why Shriji Maharaj Himself lifted Jinabhai's body when he passed away.

One should side with the devotees of God, more than one does even for one's relatives. This will earn one God's profuse blessings.

15. ABSOLUTE LOVE AND INTENSE ATTACHMENT

Our true self – the soul – is called the *atma*. The attachment one has for one's body is called *atmabuddhi*. To have the same intense attachment that one has for oneself in God and the Satpurush is also called *atmabuddhi*.

1. If a person is profoundly attached to God and His Bhakta, just as he is attached to his body, then he will not be affected by any obstacles. In fact, regardless of the extent of adverse circumstances he may encounter, he will not turn away from God and His Bhakta.

    - Vachanāmrut Gadhadā III-11

2. One should develop affection for God's Sant just as one has affection for one's wife, son, parents or brother. Due to this affection, then, the jiva becomes absolutely fulfilled.

    - Vachanāmrut Gadhadā II-59

3. Intense love for the Satpurush is the only means to realising one's ātmā; it is the only means to realising the greatness of the Satpurush; and it is also the only means to having the direct realisation of God.

    - Vachanāmrut Vartāl-11

4. If a person maintains profound love towards the Ekāntik Sant of God just as resolutely as he maintains profound love towards his own relatives, then the gateway to liberation opens for him.

    - Vachanāmrut Gadhadā I-54

5. Protect us from māyā in the form of I-ness and my-ness, and may we develop love for You. May we also have the company of the Sant who has transcended māyā and has love for You; and may we develop affection and a sense of

mine-ness towards him as well.' Therefore, we too should do the same and ask for the same, as well as do shravan, manan *and* nididhyās *on this principle.*

- Vachanāmrut Gadhadā III-39

Story 1

"Gunatit, Wake Up!"

Through dedicated service and devotion, Pragji Bhagat pleased Gunatitanand Swami. Seeing his immense faith and determination, Swami showered his grace upon him.

Once, Gunatitanand Swami instructed Balmukund Swami to call Pragji Bhagat. Within a few minutes Balmukund Swami returned, saying, "Swami! Pragji Bhagat is sleeping." Swami told him to go again to wake Pragji Bhagat up. Again Balmukund Swami went to Pragji Bhagat. He called out several times to wake him up, but Pragji Bhagat remained sound asleep.

So again, Balmukund Swami returned and told Swami that Pragji Bhagat was in deep sleep and not responding to his calls. So Swami asked, "By what name did you call him?"

Balmukund Swami replied, "I shouted, 'Wake up Pragji, wake up Pragji,' but he did not respond."

With this, Swami said, "Pragji has ceased to exist long ago. Now go and call out 'Gunatit wake up' and he'll respond immediately."

Balmukund Swami did as instructed and as he called out 'Gunatit, wake up!', Pragji Bhagat got up.

In all three states – waking, dream and deep sleep – Pragji was one with the Gunatit Satpurush.

One who has intense attachment (*atmabuddhi*) with the Satpurush remembers him in all the states. With such *atmabuddhi*, no trace of worldly attachment remains.

Story 2

Are You Attached to the Satpurush?

One afternoon in Junagadh, Gunatitanand Swami was bathing. From the nearby stables, he could hear the continuous neighing of a horse. Swami called Balmukund Swami and asked, "Why is this mare making such a noise?" Balmukund Swami went to enquire and returned with an interesting story. He said, "Swami, another mare which had been tied with it in the stables for nine days was sold this morning. Hence, out of its attachment to her, the mare is lamenting the separation"

Having heard this, Swami asked, "How many years have you been in Satsang?"

Balmukund Swami replied, "Fourteen."

Swami asked, "Have you as much attachment for the Satpurush as this mare has for her friend? Without attachment to the Satpurush, you cannot gain peace, happiness or virtues."

Balmukund Swami resolved to develop his *atmabuddhi* towards Gunatitanand Swami.

Attaching one's soul to the Satpurush is the best and easiest way to earn salvation.

16. GNAN: MAHATMYA-GNAN

Gnan means knowledge and *mahatmya-gnan* means knowledge coupled with the glory of God.

1. *Whoever realises such* gnān *of God, even if he has only a feeble intellect, should still be regarded as possessing much intellect.*

    - Vachanāmrut Gadhadā II-14

2. *The ultimate* gnān *is to know this Sadhu.*

    - Swāmini Vāto: 5.7

3. *For one who is at peace within but flares up by another's words, the remedy is* gnān.

    - Swāmini Vāto: 1.314

4. *And what is* gnān? *True* gnān *is when one's attitude is unaffected by listening to [contradictory] scriptures or talks by others.*

    - Swāmini Vāto: 1.231

5. *This sadhu is different from others. He has the virtues of* dharma, gnān, vairagya, bhakti, *etc., is* gunātit *and eternally beholds Maharaj and [through him] we have attained Maharaj Himself. To understand this glory is* gnān.

    - Pramukh Swami Maharaj

Story - 1

Bhagatji Maharaj's Wish

During his *vicharan*, Aksharbrahma Gunatitanand Swami arrived in Sarangpur. Pragji Bhagat was also with him.

Once, Gunatitanand Swami went to Narayan Kund for a bath. There, Pragji Bhagat helped Swami wash his hands with clean water. Suddenly Swami said, "Pragji! I have a lot of *gnan* stored in my heart. But there is no suitable recipient for it."

Pragji Bhagat said, "Swami! Will you give that *gnan* to me?"

Seeing Pragji's genuine spiritual thirst, Swami said, "Pragji, this *gnan* cannot be attained that simply. Only one who is prepared to sacrifice everything, control his *indriyas* absolutely and stay under my supervision can attain it."

Pragji Bhagat was prepared to meet these standards. He obeyed Swami's wishes sincerely and with the blessings of Gunatitanand Swami attained the highest spiritual *gnan*.

To attain the knowledge of God's divine form, one has to please the Gunatit Satpurush by observing his wishes in thought, word and deed.

Story 2

The Glory of Akshar and Purushottam

To promote and preserve the eternal *gnan* of Akshar and Purushottam, Shastriji Maharaj began the task of building magnificent mandirs.

He toured the villages to coordinate the work of constructing the mandirs and also to spread the true philosophy of Akshar and Purushottam through his spiritual discourses.

One day, in Ahmedabad, a devotee occupied Shastriji Maharaj's seat and began to deliver a discourse. Some devotees disapproved of this. Afterwards, they complained to Shastriji Maharaj, "This devotee sat on your seat to deliver the discourse..."

Shastriji Maharaj interrupted, "Even if someone sits on my head and sings the glory of Akshar and Purushottam I will not mind." These words of Shastriji Maharaj cleared everyone's doubts.

The *gnan* of Akshar and Purushottam is true. It is our service to explain to others this true philosophy.

17. GNAN: ATMANISHTHA

There are two aspects of *gnan*.
1. *Gnan* is to fully understand the true glory of God and His Gunatit Satpurush.
2. *Gnan* is to realise one's true form as *atma* – separate from the body. This is called *atmanishtha*.

1. Ātmā-*realisation should be of the following type: 'I am* chaitanya, *while the body is* jad; *I am pure, whereas the body is the embodiment of* narak; *I am imperishable, while the body is perishable; I am the embodiment of bliss, whereas the body is the embodiment of misery.' In this manner, when one realises the* ātmā *to be totally distinct from the body in every way, one will never consider oneself to be the body nor will one harbour affection for* vishays.

    - Vachanāmrut Sārangpur-1

2. *One should clearly understand, 'I am the* ātmā, *and not a single one of my characteristics can be found in the body. Moreover, not one of the characteristics of the body – which is* jad, *full of misery and perishable – can be found in me since I am* chaitanya.' *After making such a distinction and becoming totally free of worldly desires, one should believe oneself to be* chaitanya *and contemplate upon Purushottam Bhagwān. Discerning between that which is* jad *and that which is* chaitanya *in this manner should be known as true wisdom.*

    - Vachanāmrut Sārangpur-4

3. *The distinction between* ātmā *and non-*ātmā *cannot be realised by merely understanding the distinction as given in the scriptures; nor can it be realised by listening to discourses from a senior sadhu and deciding in one's mind, 'I shall now distinguish between* ātmā *and non-*ātmā.' *Rather, it is the extent of a person's faith in his Ishtadev –*

God – that determines how much distinction between ātmā and non-ātmā he cultivates. In fact, without using the strength of his Ishtadev, no spiritual endeavours can be fulfilled.

– Vachanāmrut Gadhadā I-56

4. *One who delivers discourses, sings devotional songs, yet does not believe that the body is not one's true form, should continually remember that 'I am not this body. I am atma, brahma, akshar residing in the body. And within me Paramatma Parabrahma Purushottam eternally resides. What is He like? He is the avatari of all avatars, the cause of all causes and above all. And He is the manifest form that I have attained." In this talk,* sānkhya *and* yoga *are both incorporated.*

– Swāmini Vāto: 1.342

5. *Ordinary* atmanishtha *is when one is not affected by insults and does not succumb to bodily comforts. What is firm* atmanishtha? *To maintain unbroken communion with Brahma; to believe Brahma to be one's true form.*

– Yogiji Maharaj

Story 1

"I Am Atma!"

Shriji Maharaj was seated under a mango tree at Parvatbhai's farm in Agatrai. There, a young boy of the *harijan* caste came. He bowed to Maharaj and Maharaj asked him, "Who are you?"

"Maharaj, I am a *harijan*," he replied.

Maharaj said, "You are not a *harijan*. You are *atma*. So repeat, 'I am atma.'"

However, the boy insisted, "But Maharaj! I am a *harijan*."

So Maharaj made him repeat 'I am *atma*' five times. But when Maharaj asked him, the boy replied, "I am a *harijan*."

Again, Maharaj made him repeat 'I am *atma*' many times, yet whenever asked, the boy always replied, "I am a *harijan*."

Eventually the boy replied, "Maharaj, I say 'I am *atma*' only because You tell me too. But I am in fact a *harijan*."

Maharaj turned to the devotees and said, "See how deeply ingrained this misunderstanding is in this boy. His *atma* has identified itself totally with his body and caste."

God and His sadhu teach us that our true form is *atma*, *akshar* – separate from the body, caste and base instincts.

Story 2

With Atmanishtha There Is No Pain

Yogiji Maharaj was in Gondal. At that time he was suffering from toothache which was giving him a lot of pain and trouble. When his attendant sadhus checked his mouth, they saw pus in his gums. Immediately they took him to the dentist.

The dentist examined his mouth and without numbing the area began to squeeze out the pus. He applied a lot of pressure and removed the pus. During this entire process, Yogiji Maharaj did not shriek even once in pain.

The dentist, who knew how painful this process could be, was surprised that Yogiji Maharaj did not experience any pain. So he asked, "Bapa, an infection like this is extremely painful. And even though I squeezed very hard, did you not experience any pain?"

Smilingly, Yogiji Maharaj replied, "Pain affects the body. There is no pain when one behaves with *atmanishtha!*"

The dentist was amazed at Yogiji Maharaj's high spiritual state.

The Satpurush is beyond the influence and attachment of the three states and the three bodies.

Yogiji Maharaj was such a Satpurush.

Story 3

Atmanishtha Personified

Once, Yogiji Maharaj visited Mojidad. There, he sanctified the homes of the devotees. He tolerated much physical hardship to please the devotees and then reached Limbdi late at night.

Having witnessed Yogiji Maharaj's hardships, the devotees and sadhus became filled with sympathy and sentiment. However, Swamishri calmed them, saying, "I used to tour here a lot before. In winter, I never used a blanket and bathed in cold water. In the monsoon, we got soaked in the rain and still visited the villages. For 30 years, I never wore slippers."

Swamishri spoke with fluent momentum. Each word echoed his elevated state of *atmanishtha*. Swamishri was the personified form of *atmanishtha*!

Atmanishtha is not a topic for mere discussion, but one that has to be practised.

The characteristics of *atmanishtha* prescribed in the scriptures are clearly evident in the life of the Satpurush.

Today, Pramukh Swami Maharaj's life reveals the ideals of *atmanishtha*.

18. VAIRAGYA

Detachment from the body and worldly objects is called *vairagya*.

1. *A person who has the highest level of* vairāgya *engages in worldly activities, either by God's command or as a consequence of his* prārabdha *karmas. But, like King Janak, he is not affected by those activities. He may indulge in the most alluring of the* panchvishays – *sights, sounds, smells, tastes and touch – attained as a consequence of his own* prārabdha, *but he does so dejectedly and with total indifference towards them. Those* vishays *are unable to entice him; thus, his renunciation remains undiminished. He invariably views those* vishays *as flawed and treats them like enemies. Moreover, he constantly remains in contact with* sadhus *and the sacred scriptures, and remains in the service of God. Even if he were to encounter adverse places, times, company, etc., his understanding would not diminish. Such a person is said to possess the highest level of* vairāgya.

   - Vachanāmrut Gadhadā I-2

2. *Upon hearing the words of the scriptures and the* satpurush, *developing an obsession that does not diminish once developed is the only cause for* vairāgya; *there is no other cause.*

   - Vachanāmrut Kāriyāni-7

3. *A devotee in whom firmness in* vairāgya *is predominant has a persistent dislike for all worldly objects, but not towards God's form.*

   - Vachanāmrut Gadhadā I-47

4. *The* vairāgya *generated by such knowledge of* ātmā *and* Paramātmā *is such that it eradicates desires of the pleasures of all* vishays.

   - Vachanāmrut Sārangpur-1

5. *If a person has a deficiency of* vairāgya, *then even if he has the* shraddhā *to eradicate his* swabhāvs, *still they will not be eradicated.*

- *Vachanāmrut Gadhadā II-7*

Story 1

Dosabhai of Bandhiya

Dosabhai, who lived in Bandhiya, was a very staunch devotee of Shriji Maharaj. Many Jain *Vanias* also lived in the village. Once, a group of them had to go to another town to attend a marriage ceremony. On the way they arrived at Gadhada. So, they went to the *darbar* of Dada Khachar to have the *darshan* of Shriji Maharaj.

Maharaj welcomed them all and enquired about Dosabhai. One of the V*anias* replied, "Maharaj, we are upto our neck in our business and worldly duties. But your Dosabhai is totally submerged. He's always busy selling *gor* from his cart. In fact, he finds time to brush his teeth only after mid-morning."

Maharaj laughed and replied, "What if we make Dosabhai into a sadhu?" The V*anias* chatted among themselves and said, "If Dosabhai becomes a sadhu, we will become *satsangis*." Then they left, promising to return on their way home.

Meanwhile, Maharaj sent a letter to Dosabhai instructing him to renounce all his responsibilities and come to Gadhada immediately. When he arrived, Maharaj initiated him into the sadhu-fold.

A few days later, the *Vanias* returned. They couldn't believe their eyes when they saw Dosabhai in the garb of a sadhu. Convinced, they said, "Maharaj, indeed Dosabhai is a true devotee of Yours. He truly possesses *vairagya*. Only then is such renunciation possible."

The devotees of Shriji Maharaj were aloof from worldly attachments. They possessed *vairagya* and offered devotion.

Story 2

Above the Attachment of Family

Lalji Suthar of Shekhpat was a devotee of Shriji Maharaj. Maharaj once visited the house of this well-to-do devotee and expressed his wish to cross the Rann of Kutch to reach Bhuj. Lalji volunteered as His guide. In the harsh conditions of the desert, Maharaj tested Lalji. Maharaj made him give away the food he had brought to a beggar, the water he carried to a thirsty passer-by, and the money he had to a thief!

After a long journey, the tired, thirsty and hungry Lalji arrived with Maharaj at the outskirts of the village of Adhoi. Here, Maharaj instructed, "Lalji, go into the village and beg for some food for us to eat."

Lalji thought for a while and replied, "Maharaj! My in-laws live in this village. Everyone here knows me. So, how can I beg here?"

Maharaj smiled and offered, "Lalji! What if I give you a disguise so that you are not recognised?"

Lalji understood Maharaj's line of thought. Immediately, he agreed to renounce and became a sadhu. Maharaj initiated him.

In his new saffron robes, he went directly to the house of his in-laws to beg alms. His wife saw him and tried her utmost to persuade him to return. However, Lalji boldly replied, "Now my spirit of *vairagya* will not be dampened."

Maharaj, too, was pleased by Lalji Suthar's staunch *vairagya* and said, "You have truly renounced your *kul* (family) and become *nishkul* (above family attachment). Therefore, your name from now onwards is Nishkulanand Swami."

Sadguru Nishkulanand Swami was the embodiment of *vairagya*. No worldly attractions ever tempted him to slacken in his observance of *vairagya*.

We bow with great respect to Nishkulanand Swami, the embodiment of *vairagya*.

Story 3

Devji Bhagat of Nenpur

Devji Bhagat of Nenpur was a faithful disciple of Shriji Maharaj. He had a thriving farm, a virtuous and youthful son, was well respected in the community and lived a *satsang*-centred life. Devji Bhagat and his wife were intensely attached to Satsang – this was their true identity. Even their young 16-year-old son was blessed with the constant *darshan* of Shriji Maharaj's divine *murti*.

As he had come of age, Devji Bhagat began to receive marriage proposals for his son. However, like his father, Devji Bhagat's son, too, was unattached and uninterested in worldly pleasures. He prayed, "Maharaj, please accept me in your service and save me from the web of *maya*." After a while, Devji Bhagat's young son passed away.

Devji Bhagat was made of a unique spiritual mettle. Instead of mourning he said, "Maharaj has taken my son in His service. That is not something to mourn about." So, he decided immediately to hide away in the farm and told his wife to take a large pot of ghee for Maharaj to Gadhada. His relatives felt that he had no worldly sense at all. Meanwhile his wife reached Gadhada and presented the ghee to Maharaj. He asked, "Is Bhagat happy?"

She replied, "Maharaj, he was happy and now he is even happier." Maharaj enquired further and she narrated the whole story. Maharaj praised Devji Bhagat's *vairagya*. Such detachment earned Devji Bhagat a place among the foremost disciples of Shriji Maharaj.

19. BHAKTI

To become engrossed with love in God, to offer through mind-words and deeds the nine forms of service; to worship God. This is *bhakti* or devotion.

1. *Mahātmya-gnān yugbhuri sneho bhaktischa mādhave.*

    "*Bhakti* is affection for God together with a knowledge of His divine glory."

    - Shikshāpatri: 103

2. *A person whose heart is filled with* bhakti *towards God feels, 'I want to act only according to God's and His Sant's commands.' Such is the spirit within his heart. Moreover, he never – even by mistake – utters, 'I will only be able to follow certain commands, but not others.'*
    Furthermore, such a person remains determined to behold God's form in his heart. If, while meditating on that form, it cannot be beheld, he does not lose courage.

    - Vachanāmrut Gadhadā I-15

3. Bhakti *of God coupled with the knowledge of His greatness is the greatest and most steadfast means to eradicate one's worldly desires.*

    - Vachanāmrut Sārangpur-5

4. *For a devotee of God, if* gnān *of the* ātmā, vairāgya *or* dharma *are a hindrance in his* bhakti *towards God, then he should suppress even them and thereby maintain the predominance of* bhakti *only.*

    - Vachanāmrut Gadhadā II-26

5. *The mind is conquered by the nine types of* bhakti *coupled with the knowledge of God's greatness.*

    - Vachanāmrut Gadhadā III-11

6. *In fact, adopting the path of* prāvrutti *in order to serve God and His devotees is the very definition of* bhakti.

                                        - Vachanāmrut Vartāl-17

7. *Thus, I very much prefer one who offers* bhakti *with* shraddhā *and without jealousy.*

                                        - Vachanāmrut Gadhadā II-52

8. Nirdosh-buddhi *is* bhakti.

                                        - Yogiji Maharaj

9. Nine forms of *bhakti*:
   Shravanam kirtanam vishnoho smaranam pādasevanam
   Archanam vandanam dāsyam sakhyamātmanivedanam

                                        - Shrimad Bhāgvat: 7/5/23

"To listen to the discourses of God, sing His kirtans, remember His exploits, offer service to Him, worship Him, honour Him, be His servant, be His friend and sacrifice oneself for Him are the nine forms of *bhakti*."

Story 1

In a Flash of Lightning

It was the monsoon season. Shriji Maharaj, together with Gunatitanand Swami, Muktanand Swami, other sadhus and devotees were in Gadhada. Daily, the sadhus listened attentively to Maharaj's discourses.

One day, after the discourses, Maharaj went to deliver a discourse to the women devotees.

It was a dark rainy night, with the occasional bolt of lightning illuminating and deafening the sky. In the middle of the night Muktanand Swami woke up and came out of the sadhus' residence. As he looked into the night, he saw a lone dark figure standing under the roof. He called out, "Who's standing there?"

"It's me, Gunatitanand," came the reply.

"Why are you standing here late at night in such weather?" asked Muktanand Swami.

Gunatitanand Swami replied, "Maharaj has gone to the *darbar* for discourses. I'm standing here so that when He returns, I can get His *darshan*."

Muktanand Swami was surprised by the answer. He asked, "You have Maharaj's *darshan* all day. Isn't that enough?"

Gunatitanand Swami answered, "No, how can one ever have enough of Maharaj's *darshan?*"

Again Muktanand Swami asked, "Don't you feel sleepy? You've been soaked by the rain." Then he left, but Gunatitanand Swami stayed.

Late that night, when Maharaj was returning to His room after the discourses it was still raining. Just at that time, a flash of lightning streaked across the sky and lit the dark night. In this flash of lightning, Gunatitanand Swami's patience was rewarded by the *darshan* of Maharaj. Only then did Swami retire.

Gunatitanand Swami spent all his time engrossed in the *darshan*, company and worship of Maharaj. His devotion and love for Shriji Maharaj was supreme.

Story 2

Yogiji Maharaj's Devotion

Once, Yogiji Maharaj and Nirgundas Swami were travelling by bullock-cart from Sarangpur to Gadhada. In the scorching afternoon sun, they made their way through barren land. It was about 4 p.m. and time to offer water to the *murti* of Harikrishna Maharaj that Yogiji Maharaj served with great affection. But no river, lake or well came nearby from which he could obtain water. Yogiji Maharaj's face revealed concern and pain at not being able to offer water to his beloved Harikrishna Maharaj.

After some time, they eventually came to a small river. Yogiji Maharaj's face lit up. He told the driver to stop. First, he bathed Thakorji and then offered some filtered water. Yogiji Maharaj then began performing prostrations to Harikrishna Maharaj, asking forgiveness for the delay in offering the water.

Nirgundas Swami was touched by Yogiji Maharaj's heartfelt devotion.

Yogiji Maharaj's life was an ideal of exemplary devotion to God. He passed his entire life in the service and devotion of God. Indeed, devotion to God was his life.

Story 3

Satpurush Teaches Us Devotion

Pramukh Swami Maharaj passes each moment of every day in the service and devotion of Harikrishna Maharaj. Such devotion is, to Swamishri, the very centre-point of life.

To understand Swamishri's devotion, some questions were put to him. His answers reveal his selfless, humble and intense devotion to Harikrishna Maharaj. From them, we, too, can learn how to imbibe such devotion in our lives.

Q: How are you able to remember Harikrishna Maharaj 24 hours a day?

Swamishri: He takes so much care of us that it is natural for us to remember Him. Before Him, we are nothing. Harikrishna Maharaj is everything. We are His servants.

Q: We accept Shriji Maharaj's words that He is manifest in the *murti*, but how can we gain the conviction and realisation that you have that Maharaj is really present in the *murti* of Harikrishna Maharaj?

Swamishri: By offering devotion, this belief will be consolidated. First you have to develop faith, then realisation will follow.

Q: If during your *vicharan*, there is a delay in offering *thal* or water to Harikrishna Maharaj, then how do you know that?

Swamishri: One who is Brahmaswarup is able to know. Since, he has no attachment for his body, all his affection is focussed on God. He has no attachment for the worldly pleasures and so such a constant link with God is natural.

Q: We regard the Satpurush very highly, since it is through him that devotees enjoy the bliss of God. However, the *murti* of Harikrishna Maharaj does not talk or move, so what type of feelings should we have for Harikrishna Maharaj?

Swamishri: Even if He does not speak, still believe that God is present. Have the same conviction and feeling that you have for the Satpurush. If this understanding is perfected, nothing else remains to be done. Have the same conviction and feelings for the Satpurush and for the *murti*. The Satpurush teaches us how to offer devotion.

Every word of Swamishri's overflows with devotion, since Swamishri is himself the embodiment of *bhakti*.

20. GOD AS ALL-DOER

To believe that Paramatma, Himself, is the creator, sustainer and destroyer of all creation. This is the belief that God is the *karta* of everything – the all-doer.

1. *Understanding only God to be the all-doer is the supreme cause of liberation.*

   - Vachanāmrut Kāriyāni-10

2. *God is the all-doer of this world. However, if one does not understand Him to be the all-doer and instead believes that it is* kāl *that is the all-doer of this world, or that it is* māyā, *or that it is* karma, *or that it is* swabhāv *that is the all-doer, then one is maligning God.*

   - Vachanāmrut Vartāl-2

3. *The factors of place, time,* karma *and* māyā *can only do as much as God allows them to do; they cannot do a single thing against the wish of God. Therefore, only God is the all-doer.*

   - Vachanāmrut Gadhadā II-21

4. *When I looked within again, I realised that I am the creator, sustainer and destroyer of all of the* brahmānds.

   - Vachanāmrut Amdāvād-7

5. *If someone comes excitedly towards us, understand that everything happens by the will of my Swami. Without his will not even a dry leaf can stir.*

   - Swāmini Vāto: 1.88

Story 1 -

Fish in a Trance

Once, Shriji Maharaj went to Sardhar with some sadhus. There is a beautiful lake there on the outskirts of the village surrounded by a vast expanse of greenery. Here, Maharaj arranged an assembly. Then, He took a dip in the lake. The sadhus were enjoying this *darshan*, when they witnessed a miracle. All the fish in the lake suddenly became still and entered into a trance. They began to float on the water surface. Everyone stared in amazement at this miraculous scene.

Just then, Muktanand Swami requested, "Maharaj, these fish floating on the surface will be devoured by the birds. So please bring them quickly out of the trance."

Hearing this, Maharaj said, "Without My wish, even a dry leaf cannot move, so who will be able to kill these fish? Who can hurt those whom I protect?"

These words enlightened Muktanand Swami, and he bowed with humility and respect to Maharaj as the all-doer.

The life-force in every aspect of creation is under the control of God. Through His wish, inanimate objects gain life!

Story 2

"Shriji Maharaj's Will Prevails."

Sadguru Muktanand Swami and Sadguru Brahmanand Swami toured the villages to spread the message of Satsang. Many *bawas* were envious of the goodwill generated by Maharaj and His sadhus, so they created trouble for them. Yet the sadhus persisted with faith, courage and tolerance.

One day, these two *sadguru* sadhus were imprisoned in a room by an envious *bawa*. Resolving to cut off their nose and ears he sat outside the room sharpening his knife. Seeing this,

Brahmanand became worried. Muktanand Swami said to him, "In whose hands is it to cut off our nose and ears? Throughout the whole of creation, only Shriji Maharaj's will prevails. Whatever He does will be for our benefit. Anyway, in our past births our nose and ears had been cut off for our families, so this time they'll be cut off for Maharaj!"

Brahmanand Swami started wondering at Muktanand Swami's understanding.

In the meantime, a devotee named Raghav Jat arrived on the scene. He saw the *bawa* sharpening his knife and enquired as to why he was doing it. When he learnt that Maharaj's sadhus had been imprisoned, Raghav Jat became annoyed. He scolded and chased away the *bawa* and freed the sadhus.

In times of difficulty like this, faith in Maharaj as the all-doer brings peace to one's mind.

That is why Gunatitanand Swami has said that in times of difficulty, prostrate even to a blade of grass. Maharaj will come to your aid through even that – for throughout the whole of creation, He is the all-doer!

Story 3

Maharaj Is the All-doer

Pramukh Swami Maharaj was in Atlanta, USA. A large *satsang* assembly was in progress. Youths were enthusiastically asking questions to Swamishri and gaining valuable spiritual guidance.

One youth asked, "Swamishri, every minute of every day you are busy in a variety of duties and activities. Among this busy schedule and all the work you do, what thought remains with you at all times?"

Swamishri replied, "Maharaj is the all-doer. With this thought, despite the numerous activities, we feel at peace."

Egotism deprives one of peace. Swamishri gives credit of all the work he does and success he attains to Maharaj. The firm understanding that Maharaj is the all-doer ensures that despite

achieving so much, Swamishri is unstained by even the tiniest
trace of ego. Consequently, he continuously experiences peace.

21. GOD HAS FORM

The principle of God being *sakar* is to believe that He has a divine form, that is, God is not formless.

1. Upāsanā *can be defined as having a firm conviction that God eternally possesses a form. Even if a person becomes* brahmarup, *that conviction would never disappear. Moreover, even if he happens to listen to scriptures propounding the view that God is formless, he would still understand God to always have a form. Regardless of what is mentioned in the scriptures, he would only propound that God has a form, never allowing his own* upāsanā *to be refuted. One who has such a firm understanding is considered to possess* upāsanā.
    - Vachanāmrut Gadhadā I-40

2. *Purushottam Bhagwān eternally possesses a form, and that form is extremely luminous.*
    - Vachanāmrut Gadhadā I-45

3. *Furthermore, of all mistakes made against God, to denounce the form of God is a very grave mistake. One should never make this mistake. One who does do so commits a sin more serious than the five grave sins.*
    - Vachanāmrut Gadhadā I-71

4. *In that divine light I see the extremely luminous form of God. The form is dark, but due to the intensity of the light, it appears to be rather fair, not dark. The form has two arms and two legs, not four, eight or a thousand arms; and its appearance is very captivating. The form is very serene; it has a human form; and it appears young like a teenager.*
    - Vachanāmrut Gadhadā II-13

5. *Māru dhām chhe re Akshar Amrut jenu nām,*
    Temā hu rahu re dvibhuj divya sadā sākar

                                  - Sadguru Premanand Swami

My abode is called Akshar. And I reside there forever with divine form.

In the Vachanamrut, Bhagwan Swaminarayan has forwarded many logical reasons justifying that God is sakar. Some of the reasons are presented below.

6. *All scriptures reveal God as the all-doer. And He who is the all-doer is necessarily sakar.*

                                  - Vachanāmrut Gadhadā II-10

7. *The Shrutis also mention: 'That God looked towards māyā.' Now if God sees, does that mean that He has only a pair of eyes and nothing else? In reality, He does have hands and feet. This proves that He possesses a form.*

                                  - Vachanāmrut Gadhadā I-45

8. God incarnates on earth to redeem *jivas*. This principle of *avatarvad* is one of the primary principles of Hinduism. Only if God has a form (i.e. is *sakar*) is incarnation possible. Thus, God is *sakar*.

9. Shriji Maharaj has described the divine assembly in Akshardham. He has described all the liberated souls (*akshar muktas*) as being of human form, with two arms, etc. All *muktas* are standing before the *murti* of Bhagwan Purushottam. All their faces resemble that of Shri Hari. Even the divine light from their forms is similar to that of Purushottam.

    On the basis of this description, a splendid painting has been produced and is displayed in the Akshar Ordi at Gadhada.

    In short, Shriji Maharaj favours the understanding that God is *sakar*.

Story 1

Hurt by the Misunderstanding of
Sushka-Vedantins

On Magshar vad 14 V.S. 1878, Shriji Maharaj arrived at the residence of the sadhus in Gadhada. He took His place at the seat prepared for Him. His face revealed an intense sadness. He sat silently. He didn't call anyone nor even look at anyone! This was because He had heard a recital of the *shushka-vedantin* scriptures and their refutation of God's form had hurt Him deeply.

Noting this incident in Vachanamrut: Gadhada II-19, the *paramhansas* described Maharaj's appearance, "The white *feto* tied around His head had loosened and had come undone, yet He paid no attention to it. In this manner, He sat extremely distressed for a few minutes. Tears had begun to flow from His eyes."

Eventually, Maharaj wrote a letter to all devotees everywhere so that they do not waver in their *upasana* and *bhakti* towards God. In the letter, Maharaj stresses the necessity of understanding God as *sakar* and with this belief to offer faithful devotion to Him.

Shriji Maharaj promoted the understanding of God as *sakar*. Devotees with this firm understanding were dear to Him.

22. GOD IS SUPREME

The conviction that Sahajanand Swami is the all-powerful, supreme Paramatma. He is the incarnation of all incarnations and the cause of all causes (*sarvopari*).

1. *Moreover, this manifest form of Purushottam Bhagwān is the controller of all, including Akshar. He is the lord of all of the ishwars and the cause of all causes. He reigns supreme, and He is the cause of all of the avatārs. Moreover, He is worthy of being worshipped single-mindedly by all of you. The many previous avatārs of this God are worthy of being bowed down to and worthy of reverence.*
   - *Vachanāmrut Gadhadā III-38*

2. *One should also intensely maintain the strength of conviction in God's form; i.e., 'I have attained the very form of God who reigns supreme, who forever possesses a divine form, and who is the 'avatāri' – the cause of all of the avatārs.'*
   - *Vachanāmrut Gadhadā II-9*

3. *I went alone to the abode of Shri Purushottam Nārāyan, which transcends everything. There, I saw that it was I who was Purushottam; I did not see anyone eminent apart from Myself.*
   - *Vachanāmrut Amdāvād-7*

4. *There have been countless avatars and countless more will incarnate, but this sadhu and this God have not come before and will not come again.*
   - *Swāmini Vāto: 1.161*

5. *Just as nothing is comparable to the Sun, similarly, nobody can stand in comparison to This God. Countless avatars have incarnated and countless more will incarnate, but they all eat only what This God gives them and act only as per His wishes.*
   - *Swāmini Vāto: 5.282*

Story 1

Samadhi to Shitaldas

Shitaldas, a Brahmin, was a spiritual aspirant who was desperate to find God. Having heard the glory of Ramanand Swami, he arrived in Faneni. However, there, he learnt that Ramanand Swami had passed away only a few days before.

Disappointed, he was preparing to return when Shriji Maharaj called him. Instantly, by the grace of Maharaj, Shitaldas entered into samadhi. He saw that all the avatars and Ramanand Swami were paying homage to Shriji Maharaj. During the samadhi, Shitaldas had a wish to perform *pujan* of Shriji Maharaj and the countless *akshar muktas*.

Maharaj realised his thoughts and said, "To create countless forms of yourself take the name of each avatar in turn and wish that if they are the supreme God that you multiply into countless forms so that you may offer *pujan* to all simultaneously." Shitaldas did as Shriji Maharaj suggested, but nothing happened.

Then Maharaj said, "Wish that if Ramanand Swami is the supreme God then you multiply into countless forms." Again, nothing happened.

Finally, Maharaj said, "Wish that if Shriji Maharaj is the supreme God then you multiply into countless forms." He did as advised, and instantly, he multiplied into innumerable forms and offered *pujan* to the *akshar muktas*.

Maharaj convinced many that He was the supreme God by blessing them with samadhi. Shitaldas, too, was convinced that Shriji Maharaj is the supreme God. So, he accepted the *bhagvati diksha* from Maharaj and was named Vyapkanand Swami.

Story 2

The Cause of All Avatars

Nilkanth Varni arrived in Loj at the ashram of Ramanand Swami. Seeing the pure and virtuous lives of the sadhus, He decided to stay there.

At that time, Ramanand Swami was in Bhuj. Mayaram Bhatt went there to inform Ramanand Swami of Nilkanth Varni's arrival and deliver a letter from Muktanand Swami. Hearing this news, Ramanand Swami instructed all his devotees to go to Loj for Nilkanth Varni's *darshan.*

Lalji Suthar of Shekhpat was a staunch disciple of Ramanand Swami. Instead of going to Loj, he went to Bhuj. So, Ramanand Swami enquired, "Why have you come here? I had sent a message with Mayaram that everyone should go to Loj. So, why haven't you gone there?"

Lalji Suthar wanted to know Nilkanth Varni's greatness, so he asked, "Swami, how great is He? Is he like Dattatrey, Rishabhdev or Ramchandra?"

Ramanand Swami replied, "Just like Shri Krishna is greater than all, Nilkanth Varni is greater than even Shri Krishna. He is the cause of all avatars."

Lalji Suthar was convinced by Ramanand Swami's words and went for the *darshan* of Nilkanth Varni. He was later initiated by Shriji Maharaj and named Nishkulanand Swami. He wrote many *kirtans* and scriptures describing Maharaj's supreme glory. Ramanand Swami also convinced many that Maharaj is the supreme God.

Story 3

Supreme Glory

Shriji Maharaj's *paramhansas* toured the villages and through their talks inspired many to became *satsangis.*

Once, Shriji Maharaj kept the sadhus with Him in Loya for eight months and spoke in great detail of His true form as the supreme God. At the end, He asked the paramhansas, "When you go to the villages, how will you explain My true form to others?" Nobody answered. So, Maharaj said, "Tell the people that I am great like Dattatrey, Kapil, Narad, Shuk, Sanak and others."

The *paramhansas* nodded in agreement and took leave.

Some time later, when they returned to meet Maharaj in Gadhada, Maharaj asked them all, "What did you say about My true form to the people?" The *paramhansas* replied, "Maharaj, we explained that you are a great person like Dattatrey, Kapil, Narad, Shuk and others."

Hearing their reply, Maharaj was disappointed, and said, "You are as dumb as doves. You have stayed with Me for so long, witnessed My divine exploits and heard My discourses, yet you have not fully recognised Me? If you eat a radish and then eat many other items, the taste of radish overpowers and suppresses every other taste. Similarly, you have heard much about My glory, yet it does not overpower other talks? I am the cause of all avatars, supreme Purushottam Narayan. So, strengthen this understanding and impart it to others."

It is imperative to understand Shriji Maharaj as the supreme God and to speak about it to others is a great service to Satsang.

23. GOD'S EVER-PRESENCE

The firm belief that God and His holy Sadhu always manifest on earth in human form to redeem all *jivas* attain salvation is the understanding that God is *pragat*.

1. Whenever a jiva attains a human body in Bharat-khand, God's avatārs or God's sadhus will certainly also be present on earth at that time. If that jiva can recognise them, then he becomes a devotee of God.

   - Vachanāmrut Vartāl-19

2. If a person realises the greatness of manifest God and His Bhakta-Sant in exactly the same way as he realises the greatness of past avatārs of God such as Rām, Krishna, etc., as well as the greatness of past sadhus such as Nārad, the Sanakādik, Shukji, Jadbharat, Hanumān, Uddhav, etc. – then nothing remains to be understood on the path of liberation.

   - Vachanāmrut Gadhadā II-21

3. If a person develops conviction in the guru – who is the manifest form of God – in the same way that he has conviction in the non-manifest deities, then, as a result, he attains all of the arthas which are described as attainable.

   - Vachanāmrut Gadhadā III-2

4. This sadhu looks like any other human, but he is not. Today, we have the manifest form of God, His holy Sadhu and dharma. One who does not realise this, will have to repent later.

   - Swāmini Vāto: 4.50

5. Koi kahe Hari ho gaye, koi kahe hovanhar,
   Mukta pragat ki prichh bin, bhatakat sab sansar.

"Some say God has incarnated and gone, some say He is yet
to incarnate,
But without understanding His ever-presence [on earth],
all spiritual aspirants will have to roam aimlessly."

6.   *Pragatne bhaji bhaji pār pāmya ghana,*
                    gidh ganikā kapi vrund koti,
     Vrajtani nār vyabhichār bhāve tari,
                    pragat upāsanā sauthi moti.
                                        - *Muktanand Swami*

"By worshipping the manifest form [of God], many have attained
liberation – vultures, monkeys, etc. Even the ladies of Vraj attained
salvation, by their adulterous worship of manifest God."

Story 1

"Shriji Maharaj Himself Is Manifest"

In 1867, Karunashankar of Dabhoi went to Junagadh to
spend time in the company of Aksharbrahma Gunatitanand
Swami. The entire region of Sorath was vibrant with joy as a
result of the inspiring discourses of Gunatitanand Swami.

Karunashankar was impressed by the observance of *niyams*,
nishtha and unity in every satsangi. Their faces reflected their
spiritual bliss. Seeing the impact of Gunatitanand Swami on
them, he asked, "Swami, I have been everywhere throughout
the Sampraday to observe the state of Satsang. Everywhere it
seems that Satsang has become old and stale! But, here, why
does Satsang seem so fresh, lively and youthful?"

Instinctively, Swami replied, "Karunashankar, Shriji
Maharaj Himself is manifest here. That's why there is joy
everywhere and Satsang is so fresh and youthful."

Bhagwan Swaminarayan is present in Satsang through the
Gunatit Satpurush. Absolute faith in one's guru brings true and
lasting inner bliss.

Story 2

Jaga Bhakta Realises Maharaj's Ever-Presence

Jaga Bhakta was one of Gunatitanand Swami's foremost disciples. Once, Gunatitanand Swami left with a large group of sadhus and devotees to go from Junagadh to Vanthali. On the way, Swami recalled the divine exploits of Shriji Maharaj.

This immensely pleased the sadhus and devotees, but Jaga Bhakta became depressed. He said, "Swami, only those who've had the *darshan* of Maharaj can really enjoy these recollections. I was born after His time. Otherwise, I too, would have had the *darshan* of Maharaj."

Hearing such disconsolate words, Gunatitanand Swami spoke inspiringly, "Bhagat, Shriji Maharaj is still manifest through His holy Sadhu. The external appearance is different, but he is the embodiment of Maharaj Himself."

These words inspired Jaga Bhakta, who fully understood their implication.

In ordinary *jivas*, God is present as a witness; in the hearts of devotees, He is present as their *antaryami;* and in the Gunatit Satpurush, God is fully manifest.

Story 3

Join Your Jiva in the Satpurush

Girdharbhai of Thasra was the nephew of Gordhanbhai, Kothari of Vartal mandir. He was a genuine spiritual aspirant and from the Vachanamrut, he learnt that if one has *atmabuddhi* in the Satpurush, one is assured of salvation. He began to search throughout the Satsang to find such a Satpurush, but without success.

Eventually, in Vartal, he stood before the *murti* of Harikrishna Maharaj, installed by Shriji Maharaj Himself, and prayed daily for one month. Pleased with his heartfelt devotion,

Maharaj manifested from the *murti* and told him, "The Satpurush at present is Pragji Bhakta of Mahuva. So develop a strong bond with him." Initially, Girdharbhai doubted Maharaj's advice but Maharaj appeared again and instructed, "Keep the company of Pragji Bhakta to ensure your *moksha*." And, when Girdharbhai went to Pragji Bhakta, he felt convinced that Maharaj's words were indeed true. From then on he served Pragji Bhakta. Girdharbhai became a sadhu and was named Vignandas Swami.

If one has a firm conviction in the glory of the manifest form of God (the Satpurush), as one has for previous incarnations, then the key to salvation is at hand. For, the Gunatit Satpurush is the gateway to *moksha*.

24. AKSHARBRAHMA

Shriji Maharaj has talked about the five *anadi* tattvas on numerous occasions throughout the Vachanamrut. These five *anadi tattvas* are: *jiva, ishwar, maya,* Brahma *and* Parabrahma. Parabrahma is supreme God, Bhagwan Swaminarayan. Brahma is Aksharbrahma Gunatitanand Swami, the abode of Bhagwan Swaminarayan – Akshardham. Synonyms used in place of Brahma include: Aksharbrahma, Akshardham, Akshar, Mul Aksharmurti, Brahmaswarup.

1. *After such an* ekāntik bhakta *leaves his body and becomes free of all influences of* māyā, *he attains Akshardhām via the* archimārg.... *That Akshar has two forms. One, which is formless and pure* chaitanya, *is known as Chidākāsh or Brahmamahol. In its other form, that Akshar remains in the service of Purushottam Nārāyan.*

    - Vachanāmrut Gadhadā I-21

2. *The happiness of humans exceeds the happiness of animals; and the happiness of a king exceeds that; and the happiness of deities exceeds that; and the happiness of Indra exceeds that; then Bruhaspati's happiness, then Brahmā's, then Vaikunth's. Beyond that, the happiness of Golok is superior, and finally, the bliss of God's Akshardhām is far more superior.*

    - Vachanāmrut Panchālā-1

3. *There is nothing greater to understand. All that has to be understood is that Maharaj is Purushottam and this Sadhu is Akshar. All these* (muktas) *are also akshar whereas he is Mul Akshar and he, too, has assumed a human form and incarnated.*

    - Swāmini Vāto: 3.38

4.   *Nijātmānam brahmarupam dehatrayavilakshanam*
      Vibhāvya tena kartavyā bhakti, Krishnasya sarvadā.
                                          - Shikshāpatri: 116

"Identify the *ātmā* as *brahmarup* and distinct from the three
bodies. With this firm understanding offer devotion to God."

Story 1

True Identity

In 1812, Shriji Maharaj celebrated the Pushpadolotsav
festival in Sarangpur at the house of Rathod Dhadhal. All the
paramhansas were present on this divine occasion.

Shriji Maharaj played *ras* with them, and while dancing, He
recited some verses composed by Kabir:

"Jogiya talat janam kerā fāsalā re;
Prem pyālā jogiā, jug jug jivo so jogiā...
Koti Krishna jode hāth, koti Vishnu name māth,
Koti Shankar dhare dhyān, koti Brahma kathe gnān.
Sadguru khele vasant..."
(The verses describe the glory of a *sadguru*.)

Then, Maharaj asked the sadhus, "Who is such a *sadguru*?"
Previously, in Loj and Mangrol, Maharaj had asked this question
and had replied that He Himself was such a *sadguru*. With this
in mind, the sadhus replied, "Maharaj! You are such a *sadguru*!"

Then, Maharaj touched His stick to the chest of
Gunatitanand Swami and said, "I am supreme Purushottam
Narayan and the *sadguru* whose glory is described in these
verses is Gunatitanand Swami.

This eternal *sadguru*, Gunatitanand Swami, in the form of
Akshardham beholds Me and the infinite *akshar muktas*. There,
in Akshardham, and here, he is always with Me in My service and
has manifested to spread the true *upasana* of My supreme form."

Everyone was spellbound to hear the true glory of Gunatitanand Swami from the lips of Maharaj Himself.

This incident was witnessed and narrated by Rathod Dhadhal to Jasa Gor and Nagji Sheth. They in turn narrated this incident to Brahmaswarup Shastriji Maharaj.

Story 2

Malji Soni of Bhoyka

Once, Gunatitanand Swami went to Vartal to celebrate the Chaitra Punam festival. Both *acharyas* and many senior *sadguru* sadhus were also present. Gopalanand Swami, Nityanand Swami, Shukanand Swami and Gunatitanand Swami were seated on the dais. Malji Soni of Bhoyka garlanded them all and pointing to Gunatitanand Swami, asked Gopalanand Swami, "Who is this *sadguru?*"

Gopalanand Swami replied, "Remember I told you that I would show you Akshardham? Well, this Gunatitanand Swami is the incarnation of Akshardham. Maharaj frequently revealed him as the incarnation of His Akshardham. Therefore make sure you understand his true glory."

These words were enough to convince Malji Soni of Gunatitanand Swami's greatness.

This incident was narrated to many throughout the Satsang. To confirm the authenticity of the details, Shastriji Maharaj went to Bhoyka to hear it directly from Malji Soni himself. Shastriji Maharaj later took Yogiji Maharaj and other devotees there to hear it from Malji Soni.

Gunatitanand Swami is Mul Aksharbrahma. When this eternal truth is understood the path of pure *upasana* is opened.

Story 3

The Gift of Akshardham

Junagadh mandir was now complete. Maharaj had also performed the *murti-pratishtha*. He called Gunatitanand Swami to the front of the assembly and appointed him as the Mahant of the mandir. All the sadhus and devotees were delighted.

Then Maharaj called Kurji Dave of Akha and said, "Dave, do you remember that many years ago you came to tell us the good news that Ramanand Swami was coming form Bhuj to give us *darshan*?"

Recalling that distant time, Kurji Dave said, "Yes, yes Maharaj I do remember."

Continuing, Maharaj said, "At that time, everyone gave you gifts in return for the good news. But I had nothing to give you so I said I would give you My Akshardham. But you did not understand what I meant."

"Yes Maharaj," Kurji Dave agreed, "I did not understand at all then."

"Well, this Gunatitanand Swami is My Akshardham. I am giving him as a gift to you and the devotees of Sorath. I have not been able to give the bliss of My company to the devotees of Sorath. Therefore, I give this sadhu, who is My all, to you."

These words of Shriji Maharaj brought immense joy to Kurji Dave. All sadhus and devotees present realised the glory of Gunatitanand Swami.

On many such occasions, Shriji Maharaj revealed Gunatitanand Swami as His heavenly abode, Akshardham.

25. UPASANA: NAVYA-VISHISHTADVAIT PHILOSOPHY

The philosophy taught by Bhagwan Swaminarayan is known as Navya-Vishishtadvait. In this philosophy, five eternal entities (*anadi tattvas*) are identified. He has also established that moksha is attained by becoming brahmarup and offering devotion to Parabrahma, as His servant.

1). *Shriji Mahārāj then said, "From the Vedas, the Purāns, the Itihās and the Smrutis, I have formed the principle that* jiva, māyā, ishwar, *Brahma and Parabrahma are all eternal.*
            - Vachanāmrut Gadhadā III-10

Throughout His life, from the time He was on His pilgrimage of India to the end, Bhagwan Swaminarayan asked questions about these five eternal entities. Thus, as *satsangis*, it is essential to understand them.

A concise explanation of each *tattva* is given below, based mainly on Shriji Maharaj's words from the Vachanamrut.

Shriji Maharaj talks about Parabrahma as existing with *jiva, ishwar, maya* and Brahma. This Parabrahma Purushottam Narayan is the controller of *jiva, ishwar, maya* and Brahma. Thus, His philosophy is known as Navya-Vishishtadvait.

1. Jiva

In the Shikshapatri, Shriji Maharaj writes, "*Jiva* resides in the heart, is subtle like an atom, *chaitanyarup*, the knower and pervades the entire body from head-to-toe through its power of knowledge. It is indivisible, unpierceable, ageless and eternal. God has given *buddhi, indriyas, man* and *pran* for the *jiva* to attain *kalyan*. The *jiva* is, in essence, *chaitanya* and *sattamatra*." (105)

The *jiva* is bonded to the three bodies: *sthul, sukshma* and *karan*. Through ignorance, the *jiva* believes the body to be its real form.

However, when the *jiva* associates with God's holy Sadhu, through his guidance, the *jiva* realises the glory of Parabrahma. When the *jiva* beholds the words of God, it fully understands the body as distinct to itself and perishable. As a result of this understanding, the *jiva* attains *mukti*.

When the body is shed, such a *jiva* attains a divine and luminous form and resides in Akshardham.

There are infinite *jivas*. God assigns a body to each based on its *prarabdha karma*.

2. Ishwar

Like the *jivas, ishwar*, too, is bound by *maya*. Parabrahma effects the creation, maintenance and destruction of the universe through *ishwar*.

Our scriptures identify Pradhan Purush, Aniruddha, Pradyumna, Sankarshan, Vairaj Purush, Brahma, Vishnu, Mahesh and others as *ishwars*.

The three bodies of *ishwar* are called *virat, sutratma* and *avyakrut*.

3. Maya

Shriji Maharaj has described the nature of *maya* in the *Shikshapatri.*

Trigunātmā tamah Krishna shaktir dehatadidayoho
Jivasya chāhammamatā hetur mayāvagamyatām.

- Shikshāpatri: 106

Maya is *trigunatmak* i.e. has Rajogun, Tamogun and Sattvagun, dark and is the power of God. It is the cause of attachment towards one's body and relations. This is the nature of *maya*.

The eight *avrans* of *maya* described in the scriptures are:
(1) *Prithvi* (2) *Jal* (3) *Tej* (4) *Vayu* (5) *Akash* (6) *Ahamkar*
(7) *Mahatattva* (8) *Mul Prakruti*.

In the Vachanamrut, Shriji Maharaj has given some unique and original descriptions of *maya*.

1. Māyā *is anything that obstructs a devotee of God while meditating on God's form.*

   - Vachanāmrut Gadhadā I-1

2. *Laziness and infatuation are* māyā *itself.*

   - Vachanāmrut Sārangpur-14

3. Māyā *is nothing but the sense of I-ness towards the body and my-ness towards anything related to the body.*

   - Vachanāmrut Gadhadā III-39

4. *The sole cause behind the* jiva *attaining liberation, transcending* māyā *and becoming* brahmaswarup *is its engagement in the* gnān, *meditation, devotional songs, spiritual discourses, etc., of the manifest form of Vāsudev Bhagwān, who is Purushottam.*

   - Vachanāmrut Gadhadā II-32

4. Brahma

The fourth eternal and real entity described by Bhagwan Swaminarayan is Brahma. Brahma is the immediate support and cause of *jiva, ishwar* and *maya*, but is subservient to Parabrahma. Brahma is also known as Akshar or Aksharbrahma.

On the spiritual path, for a spiritual aspirant to attain the state of *aksharrup-brahmarup*, the guidance of Brahma is essential. In Vachanamrut Loya 7, Shriji Maharaj says, "Only one who is *brahmarup* is eligible for devotion to Purushottam."

Shriji Maharaj has said many important things about Brahma in the Vachanamrut.

1. *That Akshar has two forms. One, which is formless and pure*
    chaitanya, *is known as Chidākāsh or Brahmamahol. In its
    other form, that Akshar remains in the service of
    Purushottam Nārāyan.*
                              - Vachanāmrut Gadhadā I-21

2. *Brahma is not subject to change and is indivisible. Thus, it
    does not undergo change, nor can it be divided.*
                              - Vachanāmrut Gadhadā II-3

3. *The nirgun aspect of Akshar has an extremely subtle form,
    smaller than even an* anu, *while the* sagun *form is much
    larger than even the largest of objects.*
                              - Vachanāmrut Gadhadā II-42

4. *When Aksharbrahma pervades* māyā *and the entities
    evolved from* māyā *- the countless millions of* brahmānds *-
    it is said to be in its* anvay *form. When it is distinct from
    everything and has the attributes of eternal existence,
    consciousness and bliss, that is said to be its* vyatirek
    form.
                              - Vachanāmrut Gadhadā I-7

This Aksharbrahma is the divine abode of Purushottam
Narayan. In Vachanamrut Panchala-1, Shriji Maharaj says,
"Aksharbrahma is the abode in which God resides. It is that God
who has a divine form."

Aksharbrahma is ever-present in the service of God.
Aksharbrahma, in its other form, beholds Purushottam and the
akshar muktas.

Aksharbrahma incarnates on earth in human form. In
Vachanamrut Gadhada I-71, Shriji Maharaj says, "When God
incarnates for the purpose of granting liberation to the jivas, He
is always accompanied by His Akshardhām, His attendants –
who are formed of *chaitanya* – and all of His divine
powers....Therefore, a devotee of God should realise that the
form of God along with His Akshardhām is present on this
earth, and he should also explain this fact to others."

There is only one eternal and unique Aksharbrahma. Although superior to the other three realities, Aksharbrahma is the servant of Parabrahma. It is by the grace of Parabrahma that Aksharbrahma is able to liberate countless *jivas.*

Aksharbrahma Gunatitanand Swami was the first incarnation of Aksharbrahma. He is, therefore, known as 'Mul Aksharbrahma' or 'Mul Aksharmurti.'

It is through Aksharbrahma that Parabrahma remains manifest on earth to guide the *jivas* towards *moksha.* So, although the physical form changes, the Aksharbrahma entity, in the form of the Gunatit Satpurush, is always present on earth. So, after Gunatitanand Swami, the succession of Gunatit Satpurush is as follows: Bhagatji Maharaj, Shastriji Maharaj, Yogiji Maharaj and, presently, Pramukh Swami Maharaj.

5. Parabrahma

Parabrahma is above *jiva, ishwar, maya* and Brahma. He is divine, independent of all, the controller, all-doer, cause of everything and is devoid of any trace of *maya.*

Parabrahma is omnipresent by His *antaryami* powers. At the same time, He is always present in Akshardham in His divine, redemptive form.

Amidst that divine light I see the extremely luminous form of God. The form is dark, but due to the intensity of the light, it appears to be rather fair, not dark. The form has two arms and two legs, not four, eight or a thousand arms....It is surrounded on all four sides by groups of muktas.

                                    - Vachanāmrut Gadhadā II-13

Parabrahma, through special powers invested in *ishwar*, manifested as the incarnations of Matsya, Kachh, Varah, Vaman, Ram, Krishna and others. Thus, in essence, these incarnations can be said to be manifestations of Purushottam Narayan (Parabrahma) Himself.

Parabrahma is the cause of all avatars. He manifests on earth to redeem the infinite *jivas* and to give spiritual bliss to His devotees.

Whether in His abode in Akshardham or in human form on earth or in His omnipresent form in all and everything, Parabrahma is always divine, free of all faults, unchanging and unattached.

Shriji Maharaj describes the glory of Parabrahma in the Vachanamrut.

I would discard all of the pleasures of the vishays of countless millions of brahmānds *just for one second's darshan of that God. Moreover, if one were to gather together all of the pleasures of the* vishays *of countless millions of* brahmānds, *even then it would not equal even one millionth of a fraction of the bliss which is present in just one pore of God.*

- Vachanāmrut Sārangpur-1

Parabrahma is one and unique. Even Aksharbrahma is incapable of becoming like Parabrahma.

In Vachanamrut Gadhada II-3, Shriji Maharaj explains how one should offer devotion to Him,

"One should develop oneness with one's *jivātmā* and with that Brahma, and worship Parabrahma while maintaining a master-servant relationship with Him."

There are four aspects of *upasana* that have to be understood:
1. God is the all-doer (*karta*).
2. God is always with a divine, tangible form (*divya, sakar*).
3. God is supreme (*sarvopari*).
4. God is ever-present on earth (*pragat*).

The special feature of Shriji Maharaj's philosophy is that He emphasizes the need to 'recognise the manifest form of God and offer devotion to him.'

God is always present on earth in the form of the Gunatit Satpurush. When the manifest form of God or His holy Sadhu is recognised, a *jiva* becomes a true devotee.

The Gunatit Satpurush is identified by His virtuous life.

Presently, the Gunatit Satpurush is Pramukh Swami Maharaj. By serving him through thought, word and deed, one attains Akshardham.

GLOSSARY

acharya
: Establisher of a religious doctrine or a school of philosophy. The later *acharyas*, starting with Shankaracharya, established schools of philosophy, having written commentaries on the Vyas Sutras, the Upanishads and the Bhagwad Gita.

agna
: Instruction, order, command.

ahamkar
: 'I-ness-maker'. One of the four aspects of the *antahkaran*, characterised by its function of giving rise to the sense of self, :i.e., sense of individual existence.

akash
: 'Space/ether' or vacuum. One of the five gross elements, from which the *sthul* body of Virat-Purush, i.e., the physical world, is formed. By nature, it provides space for all *jivas*, is the cause of the internal and external activities of their bodies, and is also where the *prans*, *indriyas* and *antahkarans* reside. The strongest of the five elements since it supports and pervades all of the other four – yet remains wholly unaffected by them.

Akshar
: 'Imperishable'. Second-highest of the five eternal entities; i.e., transcends everything except Purushottam. Also referred to as Aksharbrahma or Brahma. See also other four eternal entities: *jiva, ishwar, maya,* and Parabrahma.

: In his personal form, Akshar serves Purushottam in His abode, Akshardham, and manifests as His ideal devotee, the Satpurush, on earth. Both forms are human in appearance.

: In his impersonal form, Akshar is the abode of Purushottam, called Akshardham.

	:	In his all-pervading *anvay* form, Akshar is called Chidakash.
akshar-mukta	:	A *jiva* that has attained ultimate liberation and resides forever in Akshardham with a divine body.
aksharrup	:	'Form of Akshar'. That which has qualities similar to those of Akshar. Used to describe the spiritual state of *akshar-muktas*. Highest level of faith or spiritual status is to become *aksharrup* and worship Purushottam.
anadi	:	Eternal.
anadi tattvas	:	Eternal entities.
antahkaran	:	'Inner faculty'. The complete mind which comprises of four aspects, each characterised by its individual functions: called the *man* when generating thoughts and desires; the *buddhi* when consolidating thoughts, making decisions and resolutions, forming convictions, or discriminating; the *chitt* when repeatedly contemplating or focusing; and the *ahamkar* when forming a sense of being. Normally used in the singular since all four are aspects of the one *antahkaran*, but also often referred to as being four different *antahkarans*.
antaryami	:	'Inner knower'. Power of God to reside within a *jiva*, *ishwar*, etc.
anu	:	Fundamental, universal and atom-like unit of matter. Monad. Smallest building block of creation.
anvay	:	'Not separate'. Associated. Connected. When used for God, implies immanent, i.e., inherently existing within.
artha	:	One of the four *purusharths*, allowing for the fulfillment of desires for material objects, in particular wealth.
asat	:	'Opposite of sat'. Transient, i.e., perishable,

changing and bound by the constraints of time.

ashrams : Stage of life. Traditionally in Hinduism, there are four in total, each with their corresponding duties and responsibilities. Specifically, *brahmacharya*, as a student and celibate; *gruhastha*, as a householder with a family; *vanprasth*, as an elderly advisor, literally implying 'taking to the forests'; and *sannyastha*, as a recluse, literally implying 'throwing away' or 'putting aside', i.e., renouncing the world.

atma : The pure *jiva*, distinct from the physical, subtle and causal bodies – i.e., distinct from the *indriyas*, the *antahkaran*, worldly desires, or any other traces of *maya*.

atmabuddhi : Firm belief in one's true form as *atma*. Deep attachment or identification with God, Satpurush or any person.

atmanishtha : Firm belief in one's true form as *atma*.

atma-realisation : The resoulte understanding and knowledge that one's true form is *atma*.

avatar : Incarnation of God.

avatari : The supreme avatar, the highest incarnation of God.

avatarvad : One of the fundamental beliefs of Hinduism that God manifests on earth in human form to accept the devotion of devotees.

avyakrut : One of the three bodies of *Virat*-Purush and other *ishwar*s, the causal body. Analogous to the *karan* body of the *jiva*. The body from which the *ishwar's virat* (gross) body and *sutratma* (subtle) body evolve, and is thus also considered as the *maya* of *ishwar*.

bawa : A renunciant.

bhagvati diksha : Initiation into the sadhu-fold, following which the renunciant dresses in saffron

		robes and observes strictly the vows of poverty, chastity and obedience.
Bhakta-Sant	:	Refers to the Satpurush.
bhakti	:	Devotion to God. Noted to be of nine types: (1) *Shravanam* – Listening to spiritual discourses or devotional songs related to God. (2) *Keertanam* – Singing or talking about God. (3) *Smaranam* – Remembering God. (4) *Pada-sevanam* – Serving God's holy feet. (5) *Archanam* – Anointing God with sandalwood paste, etc. (6) *Vandanam* – Bowing before God. (7) *Dasyam* – Behaving as the servant of God. (8) *Sakhyam* – Behaving as the friend of God. (9) *Ātmanivedanam* – Unconditionally offering oneself and all of one's belongings to God with absolute submission.Where the ten types of *bhakti* are mentioned, the tenth type is *premlakshana bhakti* – profound, loving *bhakti*.
bhut	:	A gross element from which the *sthul* body of *Virat*-Purush, i.e., the physical world, is formed. There are five in total –*pruthvi, jal, tej, vayu* and *akash*. They are collectively called the five *bhuts* or five *mahabhuts*.
Brahma	:	Second-highest of the five eternal entities, i.e., transcends everything except Parabrahma. Also called Akshar, Aksharbrahma or Brahman. See: Akshar.
Brahma	:	The *ishwar* responsible for the creation of the *brahmand* and the life forms within it. Part of the trinity of *ishwar*s, along with Vishnu (the sustainer) and Shiv (the destroyer), responsible for the governance of one *brahmand*. Not to be confused with Brahma, the second-highest of the five eternal entities.
brahmacharya	:	'Divine conduct'. Celibacy. For renunciants *brahmacharya* has been prescribed as

eight-fold abstinence from associating with the opposite gender in the following ways: (1) *shravanam* – listening to or of (2) *keertanam* – talking to or of (3) *keli* – frolicking with (4) *prekshanam* – intentionally looking at (5) *guhyabhashanam* – privately conversing with (6) *sankalpa* – fantasising about (7) *adhyavasaya* – thinking of (8) *kriya* – intercourse with. For householder males, *brahmacharya* constitutes renouncing all women except their wives, abstaining from sexual relations with one's wife on days of observance, and engaging in sexual relations with her only during the appropriate times.

brahmand : Individual 'cosmos' comprising of a system of 14 realms. Each *brahmand*, created and sustained by a Pradhan-Purush pair, contains a trinity of Brahma, Vishnu, and Shiv as the governing deities. The 14 realms of each brahmand are, in descending order: Satyalok, Taplok, Janlok, Maharlok, Swarglok, Bhuvarlok, Mrutyulok, Atal, Vital, Sutal, Talatal, Mahatal, Rasatal, Patal.

brahmarup : 'Form of Brahma'. Possessing qualities similar to those of Brahma. Same as *aksharrup*. See: *aksharrup*.

buddhi : 'Intellect', derived from verb-root 'budh' – to know. One of the four aspects of the *antahkaran*, characterised by its functions of consolidating thoughts, making decisions, forming convictions and discriminating. By nature, it possesses the knowledge of all objects and is also the reason for the specific knowledge which all of the *indriyas* possess. Its inherent features are doubts, conviction, sleep and memory.

chaitanya : 'Consciousness'. The substance of the *atma*. A higher consciousness that transcends the physical realm which is *jad* and *mayik*.

chaitanyarup : See: *brahmarup, aksharrup*.

chandrayan : Strict form of fasting where one's intake of food is regulated by the waxing and waning of the moon. For example, one form is to increase food intake from one morsel of food at the beginning of a new lunar month rising to 15 morsels on Punam, then decreasing again to a complete fast by Amas; or, beginning with 15 morsels of food at the beginning of a new month and decreasing to a complete fast on Punam, then increasing again to 15 by Amas. Other forms involve having only eight morsels a day, or four morsels twice a day, or merely three morsels a day.

charnarvind : Feet. Respectful term used to refer to the holy feet of God or other spiritually elevated person.

darbar : Court of residence belonging to a king or feudal ruler, traditionally with a central courtyard surrounded by rooms with verandas.

darshan : 'Seeing', derived from verb-root 'drush' – to see. To see with reverence and devotion. Term used specifically for beholding, with inner or outer vision, God, the Satpurush, *murtis*, or highly revered people with the intention of inwardly contacting and receiving their grace and blessings. By doing *darshan* properly a devotee develops affection for God, and God develops affection for that devotee.

datan : A babul stick. A thin stick plucked from certain trees and used for cleaning teeth, by

		chewing, because of its medicinal properties.
dharma	:	'That which sustains or holds', derived from verb-root 'dhru' – to sustain or hold. Universal law or principle that 'sustains' or 'upholds' the entire world. All-inclusive term used to mean righteousness, morality, religion, responsibility and duty.
	:	The practice of religious disciplines and duties, i.e., *niyams* – including honesty, *brahmacharya*, non-violence, etc. One of the four attributes of *ekantik dharma*. Sometimes referred to as the '*dharma* of the four castes and four *ashrams*', which are encapsulated in the five religious vows.
	:	*Ekantik dharma.* See: *ekantik dharma.*
	:	One of the four *purusharths*, allowing for the fulfillment of one's personal, domestic and social duties.
dharna-parna	:	A type of fast in which the devotees fast on alternate days.
divya	:	Divine.
divyabhav	:	The firm belief that God and His Sadhu are fully divine.
ekantik bhakta	:	One possessing an elevated spiritual state wherein one offers *bhakti* to God along with *dharma, gnan* and vairagya, i.e., all four of the attributes of *ekantik dharma*.
ekantik dharma	:	Collective term for the four endeavours of *dharma* (religious disciplines and duties, i.e., *niyams*), *gnan* (spiritual knowledge), *vairagya* (an aversion for worldly pleasures), and *bhakti* (devotion) coupled with the knowledge of God's greatness – the cultivating of which will lead one to become an *ekantik bhakta* who transcends God's *maya* and attains His abode. Also called *bhagwat dharma*.

feto   : Long piece of cloth twisted and tied around
                  the head as a headdress.

gnan   : 'Knowledge', derived from verb-root 'gna' –
                  to know. Spiritual knowledge leading to en-
                  lightenment. In particular, the knowledge of
                  one's *atma* and the form and greatness of
                  Paramatma.
                : Also often used to mean *atma*-realisation or
                  atmagnan.

guna   : 'Quality'. Principle quality of Prakruti, or
                  maya. There are three in total: *sattvagun*
                  ('goodness', i.e., awareness), *rajogun* ('pas-
                  sion', i.e., desires) and *tamogun* ('darkness',
                  i.e., unawareness, lethargy). All beings are
                  affected by the influence of one or a combi-
                  nation of these three *gunas* of *maya* until
                  they become *gunatit*. With respect to the
                  influence of the *gunas* on *jivas* and *ishwars*,
                  the *gunas* elicit in people's minds three dif-
                  ferent types of moods as follows: a person in
                  sattvagun is calm, placid, peaceful; a person
                  in *rajogun* is desirous, active, sensual; a
                  person in *tamogun* is volatile, lethargic,
                  drowsy.

gunatit   : 'Transcending the *gunas*'. That which tran-
                  scends the three *gunas* of *maya* – *sattvagun*,
                  rajogun and *tamogun*, i.e., that which has
                  no trace or influence of *maya* whatsoever.

harijan   : A person of low caste.

indriya   : 'Sense', through which one can 'know' and
                  perform actions – the organ of which is the
                  physical aspect of the sense, e.g., sight
                  (eyes), hearing (ears), smelling (nose), etc.
                  There are ten in total – the five *gnan-
                  indriyas* (cognitive senses) and the five

karma-indriyas (conative senses), with the *man* often taken to be the 11th. By nature, they engage themselves in their respective *vishays* and have the complete knowledge of that *vishay*. In certain cases, it may seem that no distinction is made between the physical and subtle aspects, i.e., the senses and the sense organs are referred to by the same nouns – 'eyes', 'ears', 'nose', etc. However, they are not to be confused with the *indriyas* that form the subtle body, and which are quite distinct from the physical organs. When mentioned as the 'five *indriyas*', generally refers to the five *gnan-indriyas*.

ishwar : Second of the five eternal entities. Infinite in number. Similar to *jiva* with respect to being bound by *maya* – i.e., composed of the 24 elements, having three bodies, three states, three *gunas*, desires, etc. – but involved in the processes and lordship of the *brahmands*, and thus endowed by God with greater powers. Brahma, Vishnu, Shiv and all entities greater than them upwards to Prakruti-Purush, are considered *ishwar*s.

jad : 'Non-living', inanimate. Opposite of *chaitanya*. That which is without consciousness.

jal : 'Water' or liquid matter. One of the five gross elements, from which the *sthul* body of Virat-Purush, i.e., the physical world, is formed. By nature, it binds *pruthvi* and other substances, softens and moistens all objects, satisfies and sustains all life forms, quenches thirst, subdues heat and is abundant.

jiva : 'That which is living', derived from verb-root

'jiv' – to live. Individual, embodied soul still bound by *maya* and consequently undergoes the cycle of births and deaths. Infinite in number. It has three bodies – *sthul* (gross), *sukshma* (subtle), and *karan* (causal) – and three states – waking, dream, and deep sleep. First of the five eternal entities. See also other four eternal entities: *ishwar*, *maya*, Akshar and Purushottam.

: Often used synonymously with *atma*, i.e., a pure soul distinct from all traces of *maya*.

jivatma   : See *jiva*.

kal   : 'Time'. The universal and continuous phenomenon that accounts for and gives rise to the progression of existence and events – allowing for the past, present and future – and which ultimately leads to the destruction of all things, thus often used as a synonym of death and destruction. Like *maya*, a power of God from which the *jiva* is released when he attains liberation.

kalyan   : Salvation, liberation, redemption. Synonymous with *moksha*, *mukti*.

kanthi   : Double-threaded necklace, usually made of tulsi beads, received by *satsangis* upon initiation into the Satsang Fellowship, and worn as a sign of their affiliation to God. Derived from noun 'kantha', meaning neck.

karan   : 'Causal'. of the three bodies of the *jiva*, the causal body, i.e., the *jiva's* desires or *maya* – which causes the *jiva* to take birth again. By nature, it itself is ignorance, which has been fused with the *jiva* since time immemorial. It retains the *jiva's* *sanchit karmas* and is the cause of the *sthul* and *sukshma* bodies just as a seed is the cause of a tree. See also other two bodies of the *jiva*: *sthul* and *sukshma*.

karma   : 'Action, deed', derived from verb-root 'kru' –
to do. Any action or deed – including word
and even thought – that will sooner or later
reap its consequences. Forms part of a universal, unbiased and inescapable law central to Indian philosophy linking actions
and their fruits – cause and effect – to the
very performer of the actions, via God – the
giver of the fruits of each *karma*; i.e., pious
deeds reap pleasant fruits for the performer,
impious deeds reap painful fruits for the
performer. There are three types of *karmas*:
sanchit karmas (deeds accumulated over infinite births), *prarabdha karmas* (deeds
whose consequences are already set in motion) and *kriyaman karmas* (deeds whose
consequences are in the process of being
formed). These can be explained with the
popular analogy of the various stages of
growing rice: rice harvested and stored in
the granary can be likened to sanchit
karmas; from this stock, a portion selected
and readied for cooking and eating is like
prarabdha karmas – past deeds shaping the
present events; meanwhile, new grains being sown in the fields which will yield a
fresh crop in the future, and in turn be
added to the stock in the granary, are like
the *kriyaman karmas*, i.e., current deeds
eventually being added to *sanchit karmas*
until they 'ripen' to bear fruit as *prarabdha
karmas*, either later in the present life or in
a future life.

karta   : Doer. In Hindu philosophy, God is believed
as the *karta* (doer) of everything that hap-
pens.

katha   : Spiritual talks or discourses.

kirtan   : Devotional song.
kul   : Family.

lila   : Divine exploit.

mahant   : The head sadhu of a mandir.
mahatattva   : 'Major element'. Taken to be on par with the
                chitt of the *jiva*, but on a cosmic level. First
                of the entities produced by Pradhan-Purush.
                By nature, the entire *jagat* inherently re-
                sides within it in a subtle form. It is itself
                unchanging, luminous, pure, full of pure
                sattvagun and passive.
mahatmya-gnan : Knowledge of the form of God, together with
                or full understanding of this glory.
manan   : 'Thinking', derived from verb-root 'man' – to
                think. Contemplation. Deep reflection.
maund   : Twenty kilograms.
maya   : Instrument or power of God used as the
                fundamental 'substance' of creation. By na-
                ture, it is composed of the three *gunas*, is
                both *jad* and *chaitanya*, eternal, *nirvishesh*,
                and in its dormant state – before the time of
                creation – houses all *jivas* and *ishwars*, and
                all elements. It is inspired by, controlled by,
                and dependent on God Himself. The *jivas*
                and *ishwars* must transcend *maya*, i.e.,
                eradicate it within themselves, in order to
                attain Akshardham. Third of the five eter-
                nal entities.
mayik   : Of, or pertaining to *maya*. Opposite of di-
                vine.
moksha   : Synonym of *kalyan, mukti*.
mukta   : 'Free' or 'released', derived from verb-root
                'much' – to free or release. A liberated soul.
                A resident of any abode of God who has been
                freed from a lower plane of existence to a
                more spiritually elevated state. There are

varying levels of spiritual elevation, i.e., *muktas* of Badrikashram, Shwetdwip, Golok, etc. The highest level of *mukta*, *akshar-mukta*, has attained ultimate liberation and is free from the bondage of *maya* and the consequent cycle of births and deaths.

mukti : Synonyms of *kalyan, moksha*

Mul-Prakruti : Also called *mahamaya*, Mul-maya, or simply, Prakruti. See: Prakruti.

murti : Sacred idol of God used to offer worship.

murti-pratishtha : Traditional Vedic ceremony in which *murtis*, or images, are ritually installed in a mandir.

nastik : 'Non-believer'. Opposite of *astik*. Person who does not believe in the existence of God, or more generally, one who is not religiously inclined.

: One who proclaims as false the moral do's and don'ts prescribed by the scriptures.

nididhyas : 'Constant contemplation', derived from 'ni' + verb-root 'dhyai' – to thoroughly contemplate or ponder. Constant, concentrated contemplation on a subject. Repeated deep reflection.

nirdosh-buddhi : The firm understanding that God and the Satpurush are free of all faults and are divine in every respect.

nirgun : 'Without *gunas*'. Not possessing any attributes of the three *gunas* – *sattvagun*, *rajogun* and *tamogun* – i.e., transcends all *mayik* qualities. Divine.

: Extremely subtle.

nirmanipanu : Humility.

nirvikalp : 'Without alternatives or doubts'. Adjective describing faith or state of being in which one sees only God – but no doubts or distinctions remain whatsoever, i.e., a state of perfect realisation.

nishchay : Faith.

nishkul : Without *kul* or family.

nishtha : Faith.

niyam : Moral and spiritual disciplines, and religious codes of conduct prescribed by God, the Satpurush, or the scriptures to protect a devotee on the path to God. Niyams may relate to either the observance of *dharma* or the observance of *bhakti* . Observance of *niyams* keeps the devotee fit to travel closer to God and ultimately earns the grace of God. Transgressing *niyams* causes the devotee to fall from the path of God. Bhagwan Swaminarayan has outlined the basic niyams for all of His followers in the Shikshapatri.

paksh : Support, backing for a particular side or cause.

panchvishays : The five types of objects in which the *jiva* indulges via the *indriyas* – i.e., various sights, sounds, smells, tastes and touches. See: *vishay*.

Parabrahma : Supreme God. Also called Paramatma or Parabrahma. Highest of the five eternal entities – transcending even Brahma. See: Purushottam. See also other four eternal entities: *jiva, ishwar, maya*, and Akshar.

paramhansa : 'Supreme swan'. A male sadhu of the highest order, characterised by his ability to discriminate between *sat* and *asat* – just as swans were traditionally considered to be able to distinguish between milk mixed with water. Traditionally, they renounce not only worldly pursuits but also all religious accessories such as rites, symbols and objects – daily worship, *chandlo, kanthi*, etc. – and lead a life of traveling and preaching. In the time of Bhagwan Swaminarayan, there was an illustrious legion of 2,000 learned, talented and saintly sadhus of which 500 were initiated into the paramhansa order. These were later re-initiated as sadhus and had returned to performing all traditional religious rites and rituals, but were still known as *paramhansas*.

parshad : Male renunciant in the time of Bhagwan Swaminarayan, similar to a sadhu, but one whose *niyams* were not as stringent; i.e., they observed *brahmacharya* in general but were allowed to talk with women, were allowed to touch money but not keep it for themselves, etc. Most *parshads* shaved their heads like other sadhus but wore a white – not saffron – *dhotiyu* and upper garment.

pragat : Manifest

Prakruti : 'Primal nature'. Divine energy or instrument of God that initiates the creation process by being 'impregnated' by Purush – also called Mul-Purush, Maha-Purush, or Akshar-Purush – and from which countless pairs of Pradhans and Purushes are 'conceived' for the creation and sustenance of each *brahmand*. Taken to be feminine in nature, she is composed of the three *gunas*, is both *jad* and *chaitanya*, eternal, *nirvishesh*, and in her dormant state houses all *jivas* and all elements. Also called Mul-Prakruti, Mul-maya, and even *mahamaya*. See also: *maya*.

: Also refers to Pradhan-Prakruti.

pran : 'Vital airs', derived from verb-root 'pran'– to breathe. Collective term referring to the principle life force or energy flowing within the primary life-currents of the body, called *vayus*, which control crucial bodily functions.

There are five main vayus: (1) *pran* – exhaled breath (2) *apan* – inhaled breath (3) *saman* – equalising breath (4) *udan* – ascending breath (5) *vyan* – retrained breath and five subordinate *vayus*: (1) *nag*, (2) *kurma*, (3) *kukal*, (4) *devadatta*, and (5) *dhananjay*.

prarabdha : *Prarabdha karmas*. Often loosely taken to mean fate or destiny. See also: *prarabdha karmas* and *karma*.

prarabdha karma: 'Deeds whose consequences are already set in motion'. The portion of the stock of *karmas* (*sanchit karmas*) that are presently bearing fruit, based on the principle of past deeds shaping present events. *Prarabdha karmas* influence the nature of one's body and associations, prevailing circumstances, and even personal inclinations. Also referred to as simply *prarabdha*. See also: *prarabdha* and *karma*.

prasad : Sanctified food, blessed and consecrated by having been offered to God.

pravrutti : 'Activity'. Activity in the form of social duties and affairs. In this sense, often used to refer to the path of a householder.

: Can also encompass all forms of activities and responsibilities – even religious activities such as serving in the *mandir*, attending to devotees of God, etc. – i.e., emphasising devotion and service rather than mere contemplation and meditation.

pruthvi : 'Earth' or solid matter. One of the five gross elements, from which the *sthul* body of Virat-Purush, i.e., the physical world, is formed. By nature, it supports all *jivas*, and in the form of a celestial body, is their place of residence. It separates *akash* and the other four *bhuts*, and gives a physical form

<table>
<tr><td></td><td>to all life forms.</td></tr>
</table>

	: Also used to mean earth.
pujan	: Worship.
purani	: A person reading scriptures.
purusharth	: 'Pursuits'. Collective term for the four goals legitimately pursued by all Hindus, namely: *dharma* (duties), *artha* (material wealth), *kam* (desires), and ultimately, *moksha* (liberation).
rotlo	: A basic unleavened bread-like staple food of many parts of Gujarat, made generally of millet flour that is kneaded and patted into a flat, circular shape before being cooked on an earthen or metal hot plate.
sadguru	: 'True guru'. Refers to the Satpurush. See: Satpurush.
sadhu	: Male person who has renounced worldly pursuits and has chosen an austere life of religious activities under strict vows of poverty, chastity and obedience. A Hindu renunciant.
sagun	: 'With *gunas*'. Possessing divine qualities and redemptive virtues.
	: 'With *gunas*'. Possessing *mayik* qualities, i.e., *mayik* – not divine.
sakar	: Lumps of processed sugar crystals.
samadhi	: 'Trance'. Transcendental experience, usually of God or His abode, in which consciousness of the body and surroundings is lost.
	: Eighth and final step of *ashtang-yoga*. Transcendental experience of union with God, which is the culmination and climax of yoga.
sankhya	: Fundamental belief of the Sankhya doctrine; i.e., all that evolves from *maya* is perishable and vain. Cultivating thoughts of *sankhya*, the devotee gradually becomes de-

		tached from worldly, *mayik* objects allowing him/her to become further engrossed in God.
sarvopari	:	Supreme.
sat	:	Permanent, i.e., imperishable and unchanging. Transcending time, and thus unbound by the past, the present and the future.
Satpurush	:	Guru for a spiritual aspirant. Aksharbrahma by form and the living embodiment of Parabrahma Purushottam. Through whom God remains ever-manifest, passing on His divine energy and experience, love and guidance to all beings on earth. The continuing lineage of God-realised Satpurushes ensures that the gateway to liberation and God is forever open for all seekers. Surrendering to him, striving to obey his commands, and developing profound love for him is the root of all spiritual endeavours. Synonymous in the Vachanamrut with Sant, Bhakta, Ekantik Bhakta, Ekantik Sant, Param-Bhagwat, Param-Bhagwat Sant, Param-Ekantik Sant, Purush and Sadguru.
satsangi	:	A member of the Satsang felllowship. One who practices *satsang*.
sattamatra	:	Independent, controller.
seva	:	Service.
shraddha	:	A virtue that incorporates qualities of faith, trust, hope, patience, persistence and zeal.
shravan	:	'Listening', derived from verb-root 'shru' – to listen. For example, to listen to, or do *shravan* of the talks of God.
shushka-vedanti	:	'Dry Vedanti'. One who propounds or adheres to the *shushka*-Vedanta school of philosophy. See: shushka-Vedant.
shushka-vedant	:	'Dry Vedanta'. The Advait doctrine. Monotheistic school of Vedanta propounding that the ultimate reality is only the one, 'non-

dual' Brahma. Referred to as 'dry' because it disclaims the existence of a personal God, His eternally divine form, His abode, etc., and so does not propound any form of bhakti or worship of God and His avatars.

sthitpragna : A devotee with unshakable knowledge and understanding of the divine form of God.

sthul : 'Gross', as opposed to *sukshma*, i.e., subtle. Of the three bodies of the *jiva*, it refers to the physical body of the *jiva*, which is composed of the five elements, i.e., the five *bhuts*. Includes all of the physical, visible aspects commonly referred to as the 'body'. Because it is evolved from the *karan* body, it is also considered as the *jiva's maya*. The *jiva* attains a different *sthul* body upon each birth. See also other two bodies of the *jiva*: *karan* and *sukshma*.

sukshma : 'Subtle', as opposed to *sthul*, i.e., gross. Of the three bodies of the *jiva*, it refers to the subtle body of the *jiva*, which is composed of 19 elements: the five *gnan-indriyas*, the five *karma-indriyas*, the five *prans* and the four *antahkarans*. Unlike the *sthul* body, the *sukshma* body is not visible and is commonly thought of as the mental 'body'. Because it is evolved from the *karan* body, it is also considered as the *jiva's maya*. See also other two bodies of the *jiva*: *sthul* and *karan*.

sutratma : One of the three bodies of Virat-Purush and other *ishwar*s, the subtle body. Analogous to the *sukshma* body of the *jiva*. Because it is evolved from the *avyakrut* (causal) body, it is also considered as the *maya* of *ishwar*.

swabhav : A person's vicious natures such as lust, anger, greed, jealousy, egotism, etc. Also used to refer to a person's natures in the form of

habits formed after repeated actions, in this
birth or in the one's past. The eradication of
all of one's *swabhavs* and feelings of body-
consciousness is necessary in order to attain
ultimate liberation.

tapta-kruchh : Form of stern austerity entailing fasting for
12 continuous days.

tej : 'Fire' or energy. One of the five gross elements, from which the *sthul* body of Virat-
Purush, i.e., the physical world, is formed.
By nature, it is luminous, causes the diges-
tion of food, absorbs liquids, eliminates cold,
dries, creates hunger and thirst, and burns
wood, ghee and other sacrificial offerings.

trigunatmak : Composed of the three *gunas*.

upasana : 'Sitting near', derived from 'upa' + verb-root
'as' – meaning to sit near. Philosophical
framework outlining the fundamental principles of a doctrine. Philosophical understanding of the nature of God as well as the
mode of worship of God, i.e., how one understands God to be like, and how one worships
Him. Sometimes synonymous with *bhakti*.

vairagya : 'Detachment'. An aversion or strong, persistent dislike, generally for the world and its
mayik pleasures, i.e., the *panchvishays*.
Characterised by remaining detached from
the body and the *brahmand*, or from all
things that are the products of Prakruti.
One of the four attributes of *ekantik
dharma*.

Vaniya : Specific class of people of the Vaishya caste
traditionally engaged in commercial activities.

vayu : 'Air' or gaseous matter. One of the five gross

elements, from which the *sthul* body of Virat-Purush, i.e., the physical world, is formed. By nature, it causes trees to shake, gathers leaves and other objects, carries the *panchvishays*, i.e., sights, sounds, smells, tastes and touch, to their respective *indriyas*, and is the vital force of all of the *indriyas*.

vicharan : Spiritual touring.

virat : Of the three bodies of Virat-Purush and other *ishwar*s, the physical body, i.e., the physical world itself – composed of the five *mahabhuts* – and which sustains the bodies of all *jivas*. Because it is evolved from the *avyakrut* (causal) body, it is also considered as the *maya* of *ishwar*.

vishay : An object indulged in by the *jiva* via the ten *indriyas* (senses). The five types of *vishays* – various sights, sounds, smells, tastes and touches – are called the *panchvishays*. The *jiva* cannot remain without indulging in the *vishays*, but *vishays* related to God uplift while *vishays* related to the world pollute the *jiva*. The *jiva*'s deep-rooted desire to indiscriminately indulge in the pleasures of the *vishays* deflects it from the path of ultimate liberation.

vyatirek : 'Separate'. Distinct or unassociated. Unconnected. When used for God, implies transcendent.

yoga : 'Union' derived from verb-root 'yuj' – to yoke or join. School of philosophy focusing on quieting the fluctuations of the mind through various physical and mental practices and ultimately aiming at the transcendental experience of union with God.